Doll Costume Dress Up

20 Sewing Patterns for the 18-inch Doll

Joan Hinds

KP CRAFT
CINCINNATI, OHIO

Table of Contents

Introduction

What girl hasn't envisioned being a princess, a cowgirl, or a clown? Girls can bring these visions to life by dressing their dolls in similar fashions. Halloween costumes are always fun, but doll costumes can stretch a girl's imagination throughout the year.

I have designed twenty costumes for 18" (45.7cm) dolls, ranging from Cinderella to a superhero. Several of them, such as a witch, pumpkin and black cat are traditional Halloween costumes. The hospital scrubs or ballerina costume can help with role playing in today's world. Or, express creativity and imagination with the gypsy, fairy and pirate costumes.

These costumes are created with children in mind, but you can make them more ornate or simpler by adding or removing trims and decorative stitching.

The young doll lover in your life will have her dreams come true when you create her favorite doll costumes!

Getting Started

Sewing for Your Doll

The 18" (45.7cm) doll is the most popular doll to sew clothing for. The most common brand is American Girl doll by Pleasant Company, but other manufacturers have created their own brand of 18" (45.7cm) vinyl dolls. The faces are unique to each brand, but the cloth bodies are sufficiently similar to exchange clothing, particularly dresses. Arms and legs sometimes vary enough to require different sleeve and pant lengths, but most 18" (45.7cm) doll brands will fit the clothing in this book.

Even within a single brand, the cloth bodies may vary from doll to doll. The bodies don't come from a mold and there is a human element involved in their fullness. Also, dolls that remain in stands or are actively played with may become slimmer over time. In most cases, the most critical measurement is the waist. The patterns in this book presume an 11" (27.9cm) waist. This measurement is most important when making garments with a waistband. If your doll comes from another manufacturer, take careful measurements before you start. Often the bodies will be slightly thinner, especially in the neckline and waist. Be aware that your doll may need slight adjustments in waistbands, hem and sleeve lengths.

The clothing in this book is designed to fit the American Girl doll, but it's advisable to still take a waist measurement since waist sizes may vary. With other brands, insure a perfect fit by making a trial muslin for the garment, or at least the bodice. This way you can see how well the garment will fit and which alterations you will need to make. It is helpful if you have the doll nearby while you make her clothing. Try each garment on the doll as you sew to make sure you have the proper fit.

Easy Alterations

If your doll's waist is smaller than 11" (27.9cm) around the waist, you will need to adjust the waist. If the garment has elastic in the waistband, shorten the elastic length to make it fit. You can overlap the center back edges of the bodice before you sew the hook and loop tape in place if the top is slightly larger than you would like. If the bodice or shirt is too full, trim a small amount off the side seams or the center back seam before finishing the garment.

Most dolls will not have a waist thicker than 11" (27.9cm). If you need to add width to the clothing, add a small amount to the side seams under the armholes. To widen pants at the waist, add a small amount to the width at the top of the pants pattern pieces, and be sure to lengthen the waistband.

Taking a little extra time to check the fit of the garments will insure you are satisfied with the results.

Tools and Equipment

It's always a good idea to assemble all your tools and equipment before you begin. For this book, your sewing machine will need to be capable of straight and zigzag stitches. One specialty foot you may find useful is an edge-stitching foot. This foot has a metal guide along one side of the presser foot. This guide lines up along fabric edge and will insure a straight stitching line. It can also provide you with an accurate ¼" (6mm) seam allowance for doll clothing. Make sure your machine is stocked with new needles appropriate for your fabric choices. A serger is not necessary even for knits, but it is helpful with construction and gives seam allowances a clean finish. If you don't have a serger, finish the seams with a zigzag stitch or cut the garment out with pinking shears.

A steam iron is a must. There are mini-irons available that are designed for the quilting industry but are perfect for pressing small areas in doll clothing. Small ironing boards or sleeve pressing boards are wonderful for pressing small sleeves, collars, pant legs, etc. Use a metal hem gauge to achieve a straight line when pressing fabric edges to the wrong side.

Rotary cutters, mats and rulers make cutting your fabric quick and easy. Use them to cut all the straight pattern pieces that just have measurements given. Be sure to have a sharp blade to limit frustration when cutting.

Other useful tools are sewing shears, paper cutting scissors, hand sewing needles, straight pins, small clippers, a tape measure, temporary basting spray and markers such as a chalk pencil. A bodkin to insert elastic is useful for many of the garments. Pinking shears can be used to cut out the garment for ready-made seam finishes.

Sewing Basics

Sewing for dolls uses basic and unusual sewing techniques and frequently incorporates different types of fabric. An important thing to note is ¼" (6mm) seam allowances are used in all cases unless otherwise specified.

Common methods for finishing seams are serging, zigzag stitching or using pinking shears. If you choose to serge your seams, I recommend using a 4-thread basic stitch. A serged seam finish will look the most like ready-to-wear clothing, but zigzag stitching will prevent raveled seams too. I have included the phrase "serge or zigzag stitch" when I feel a seam finish is necessary. Pinking shears are also frequently used to finish doll clothing seams. They can be used to trim the seam around curves so clipping the seam will not be necessary. Another method is to press the edge ¼" (6mm) to the wrong side and then press under another ¼"(6mm) before stitching. You will find one of these procedures in each set of instructions, but they are interchangeable. Just remember to add an additional ¼"(6mm) to the pattern pieces before cutting them out if you choose to press the edge under twice instead of serging/zigzagging as the instructions specify.

Facings are difficult to apply to doll garments since the pieces are so small. I like to use a self-lining in the bodices of dresses or tops, which is described in the project instructions.

Sewing with knits only requires a few minor adaptations. Make sure your sewing machine needle is appropriate for knits. The seams in the knit garments are quite short, which helps eliminate stretching. Use a straight or zigzag stitch on your sewing machine, or stitch the seams with a serger.

Remember, there is not one right way for construction. You can choose which technqiues work best for you, and use those in your garments. For example, choose your favorite way to close the garments. The most common way is with a hook-and-loop closure such as hook and loop tape, but substitute small snaps if you prefer. Some garments are open all the way down the back, and others have the seam in the back partially stitched. It's your choice which of these methods to use.

Adding Gathers

To gather fabric, place the fabric under the presser foot about a seam width away from the edge. Turn the wheel by hand to take one stitch. Pull up on the top thread and bring the bobbin thread to the top of the fabric. Pull both of the threads together as long as the area to be gathered and give them a gentle twist. Place the threads under the presser foot, along the edge of the fabric to be gathered. Adjust your machine for a medium zigzag stitch with a length of 3.0. Stitch over the threads just inside the seam allowance, making sure not to stitch on or through the threads. (Figure 1) Stop a seam width away from the edge. Pull on the twisted threads to gather the fabric. Since the threads were secured in the beginning, they will not come out. Secure the thread tails by wrapping them around a pin after the gathers are pulled to the correct size. (Figure 2)

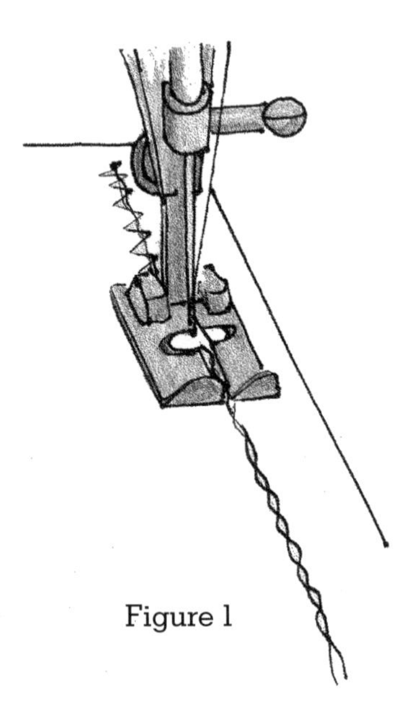

Figure 1

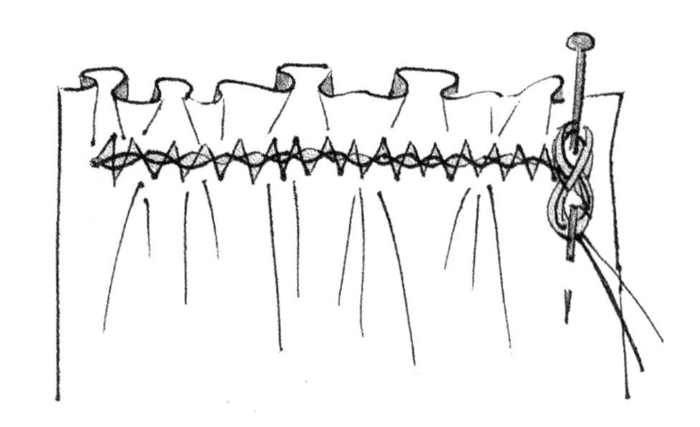

Figure 2

Sewing with Fancy Fabrics

Since many costumes are designed for special playtimes or Halloween, they tend to be made of shiny and slippery fabrics like satin, sequin knit and chiffon. These fabrics are thought to be more difficult to sew, but here are a few techniques to make stitching a breeze.

- Make sure your sewing equipment is in good working order.
- Scissors and needles must be sharp to avoid snagging the fabric.
- Use the appropriate size needle for your fabric choice.
- Cut your fabric on a flat surface so the fabric will not slip out of place. Pins may leave holes, so test your fabric before pinning.
- Place your pins in the seam allowance if they are necessary, or use a glue stick or temporary basting spray to hold your fabric in place.
- Be careful when feeding slippery fabrics through the sewing machine as the fabric may stretch.
- Raveled edges can be a problem with small seam allowances. Try a seam sealant or zigzag stitching on the edges of your cut fabric before assembly.
- Often, these shiny fabrics are made from synthetics that require a lower pressing temperature. Test iron on a scrap of the fabric to find the proper temperature before pressing your garment.

Using the CD and Patterns

All of the pattern pieces for the costumes in this book are found on the CD. To use the CD, insert the CD into a computer. Open the PDF file of the costume you want to make. Print the file on your home printer, making sure the patterns print at 100 percent and are not scaled to fit the page. All pattern pieces will print at the size you need to make the garment; you will not need to enlarge any of the patterns. For patterns that are too large to fit on one page, tape the pattern together along the dotted lines.

On the first page of each costume file is a 1" × 1" (2.5cm × 2.5cm) box. Please measure this box with a ruler to ensure that your patterns have printed at the correct size. If the box does not measure 1" × 1" (2.5cm × 2.5cm), please check the settings on your computer and printer to make sure that scaling is turned off and you are printing at 100 percent.

Any costume pieces that are squares or rectangles will not have a pattern piece on the CD. Instead, cutting instructions for those pieces will be provided in the instructions for the costume.

Useful Accessories

These accessories can add just the right touch to your next doll costume. Create a mask for your Cinderella costume to make her ready for a masquerade ball, or for your superhero to disguise her identity! The slip with hoops pattern is just right for making the full-skirted costumes seem to float.

Mask Instructions

Masks can be worn with any costume, but particularly with Halloween costumes. Here, you'll find a basic mask pattern that can be made out of any fabric to pair perfectly with any costume. You are limited only by your imagination. Now, let the fun begin!

Mask Supplies:

Mask pattern pieces: Mask

3" × 5" (7.6cm × 12.7cm) scrap of felt or fabric

3" × 5" (7.6cm × 12.7cm) scrap of interfacing

8" (20.3cm) elastic, ¼" (6mm) wide

1 Cut one mask shape from sturdy fabric, such as felt, and one from interfacing. Iron interfacing to the back of the mask for stability.

2 Stitch one end of an 8" (20.3cm) piece of elastic securely on either side of the mask at the marks on the pattern piece. (Figure 1)

3 Decorate the edge of the mask with sequins or trim. Add feathers, buttons, jewels or beads to make your mask extra special and unique.

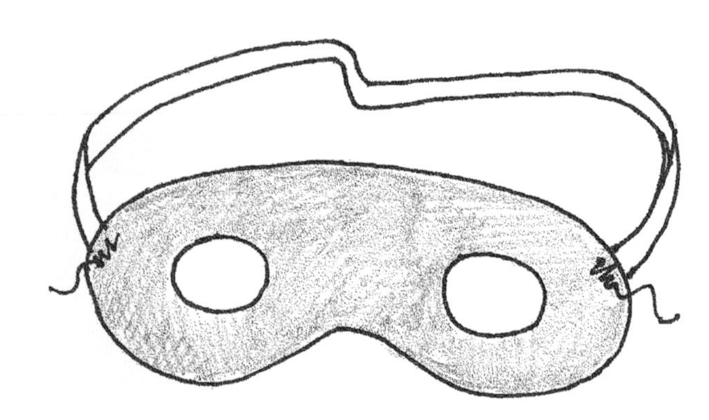

Figure 1

Slip with Hoops Instructions

This structural undergarment adds a touch of historic charm to many of the costumes in the book.

Slip with Hoops Supplies:

12¾" × 36" (32.4cm × 91.4cm) rectangle of white broadcloth

11½" (29.2cm) elastic, ¼" (6mm) wide

2¼ yards (2.1m) of covered plastic boning

1 Stitch the short ends of the fabric together. Press seam allowances open.

2 Press one long edge of the fabric ½" (13mm) to the wrong side. Press under another ½" (13mm) and stitch in place.

3 Press the opposite edge ¼" (6mm) to the wrong side. Press under another ½" (13mm) and stitch, leaving a couple of inches open at the seam for a casing.

4 Cut the boning in half. Working on the wrong side of the fabric, draw a pencil line around the full circumference of the dress, 1" (2.5cm) up from the hemline. Place one side of the boning along the drawn line. Begin a few inches before the seam and stitch along one edge of the boning. When you reach the end, overlap the boning ends and continue stitching to complete the circle. (If the boning does not overlap, it will not make a smooth circle.)

5 Stitch the remaining boning 2" (5.1cm) above the first row, following the instructions in step 4. (Figure 2)

6 Insert elastic in the casing and stitch the ends together overlapping slightly. Stitch the opening closed.

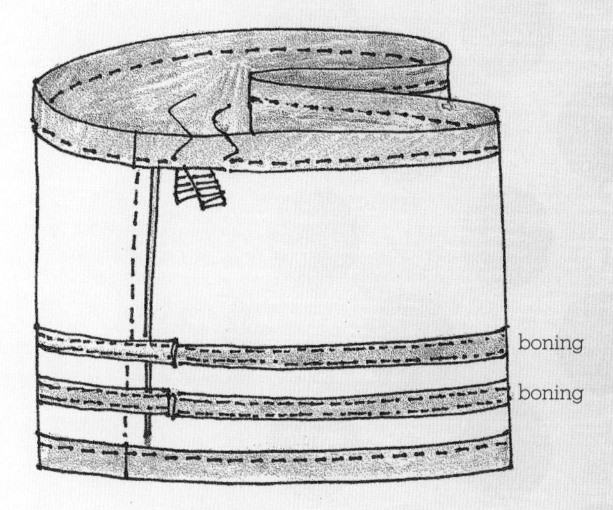

Figure 2

Fun & Fancy

Lilac Fairy

Leotard, Skirt, Wings and Wreath

Girls love to pretend to be a fairy, and your doll can be one, too. This skirt is made from four colors of netting. Purchase it in 6" (15.2cm) wide rolls in craft or party stores to make it easy. The leotard, also made for the *Ballerina* costume, needs to be constructed from very stretchy fabric such as swimsuit knit or Lycra. The straps and top edges are made from fold-over elastic strip, which is a newer sewing product. Decorate the front of the leotard with your choice of floral trim. Substitute bias tape for the floral tape in the wreath if you prefer.

Leotard Supplies

- *Lilac Fairy* pattern pieces: Leotard Front, Leotard Back
- ¼ yard (0.2m) Lycra knit fabric
- 9½" (24.1cm) elastic, ⅛" (3mm) wide
- ⅔ yard (0.6m) fold-over elastic, ⅝" (16mm) wide
- 4" (10.2cm) strip of hook and loop tape, cut in half lengthwise

Skirt Supplies

- 2½" × 16" (6.4cm × 40.6cm) satin fabric
- 2½" × 16" (6.4cm × 40.6cm) sheer fabric
- 3 pieces of 6" × 54" (15.2cm × 137.2cm) netting in four colors (can be purchased on 6" [15.2cm] wide rolls)
- 10½" (26.6cm) elastic, ¼" (6mm) wide

Wings Supplies

- *Lilac Fairy* pattern pieces: Wing
- pencil or water-soluble marker
- (2) 12" (30.5cm) squares of white netting
- covered bridal wire for wings, 30-gauge

Wreath Supplies

- assortment of 18–20 flowers or sprays (picks) with wire stems, 1"–1½" (2.5cm–3.8cm) wide
- 13½" (34.3cm) covered wire for wreath, 18-gauge
- white floral tape or white bias tape
- fabric glue

Leotard Instructions

1 Cut one front and two backs from the Lycra knit fabric. With right sides together, sew the center back seam up to the dot marked on the pattern piece. Fold the unstitched part of the seam allowances ¼" (6mm) to the wrong side and topstitch. (Figure 1)

2 Cut a 4¼" (10.8cm) piece of the fold-over elastic to fit across the top edge of the front. Fold the elastic in half over the edge and zigzag stitch in place. (Figure 2)

3 Cut two 2¾" (7cm) pieces of the fold-over elastic for the top of each back. Fold the elastic in half over the back edge, turning in the ends at the center back before stitching.

4 Cut two 6¼"(15.9cm) pieces of the fold-over elastic. Beginning at one of the front side seams, fold the elastic over the armhole and pin.

5 Measure 2¾" (7cm) away for the strap. Begin pinning the elastic again over the armhole, and end at the back side seam. Zigzag the entire length of the elastic.

6 Sew the side seams with right sides together. (Figure 3)

7 Cut the ⅛" (3mm) elastic piece in half. Stretch a piece around the inside of each leg opening. The ends of the elastic should be flush with the fabric edges. Serge or zigzag the elastic to the legs. Roll the elastic toward the inside of the leotard and zigzag stitch.

8 With right sides together, stitch the inseam. (Figure 4)

9 Overlap one side of the center back by ¼" (6mm) and sew the 4" (10cm) strip of hook and loop tape to each side. (The other half of the 4" strip is not used.)

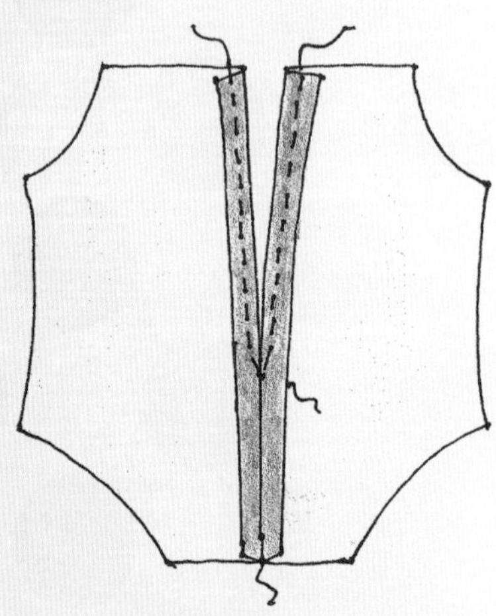
Figure 1

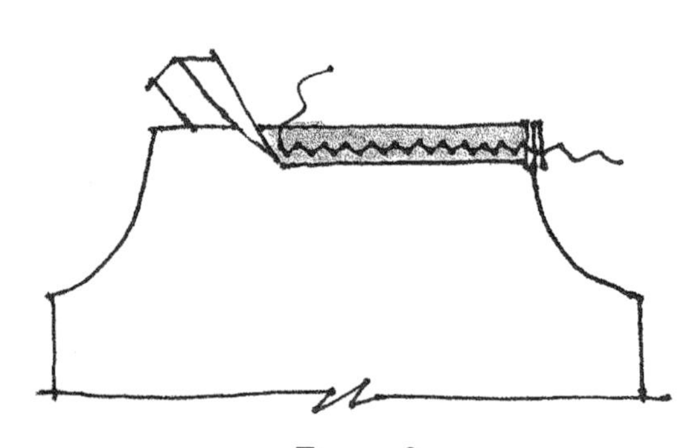
Figure 2

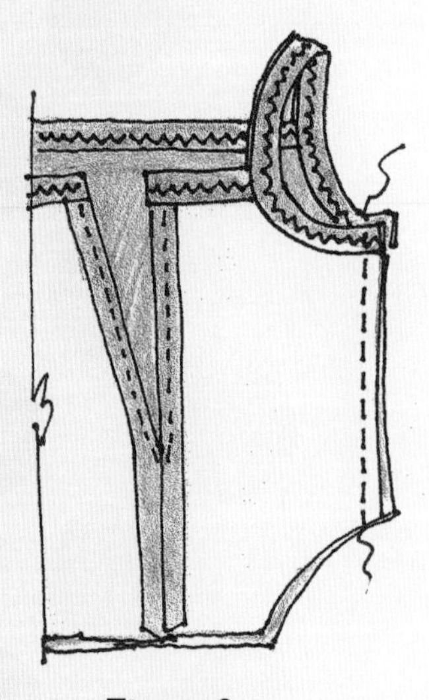
Figure 3

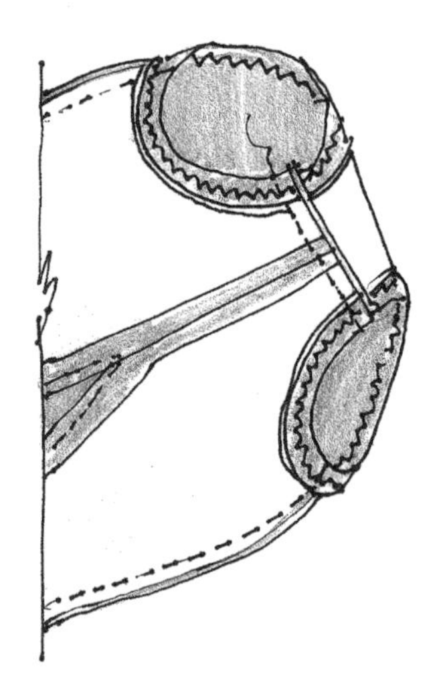
Figure 4

Skirt Instructions

1 Place the sheer fabric over the right side of the satin fabric; baste to hold. Fold them in half lengthwise and serge or zigzag stitch the raw edges together. Stitch ½" (13mm) away from the fold to make a casing. (Figure 5)

2 Cut the netting into 18" (45.7cm) pieces. Fold each netting piece in thirds so each section measures 6" (15.2cm) square.

3 Gather the squares by taking one stitch at the top of one of the squares and pulling up the bobbin thread. Pull out the bobbin thread at least 2 yards (1.8m). Place the thread along the top edge of the square. Zigzag over the bobbin thread, adding another square of netting as you finish the first one. Continue with all twelve squares. (Figure 6)

4 Pull the bobbin thread so that the gathered edge of the netting is the same width as the serged edge of the satin skirt piece. With right sides together, stitch the netting to the skirt. (The stitching will be underneath the skirt when finished.)

5 Insert the elastic in the casing and secure it at each end. (Figure 7) Fold the netting down and stitch the center back seam of the skirt.

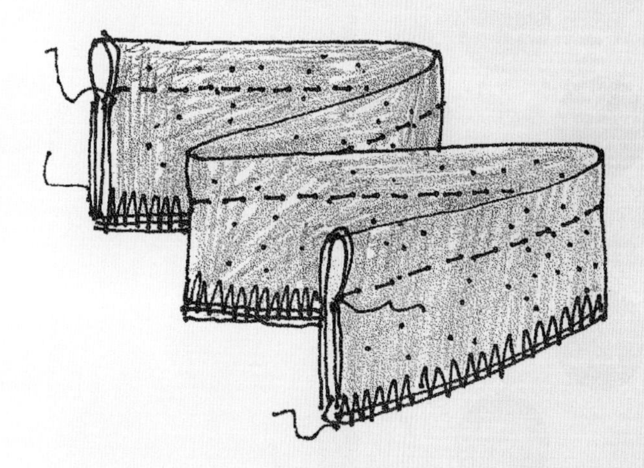

Figure 5

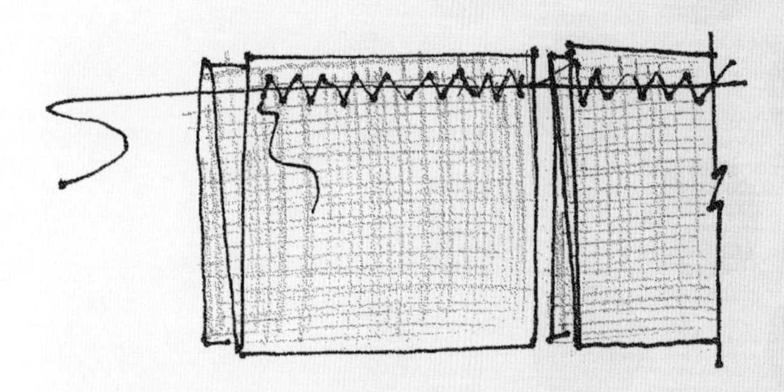

Figure 6

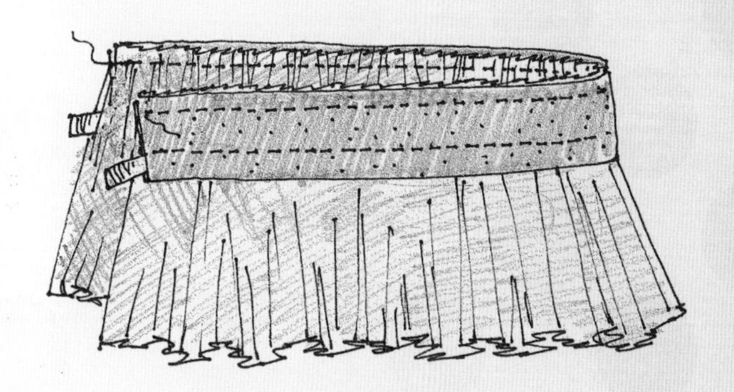

Figure 7

Wings Instructions

1 With a pencil or water-soluble marker, trace the wing pattern on one side of a piece of white netting. Flip the pattern over and trace a mirror-image wing that joins with the first one between points.

2 Pin the marked netting to another square of netting. Arrange the wire so that it follows the lines of each wing, overlapping the ends. Zigzag the wire to the two wings. (Figure 8)

3 Cut the wings out of the squares, outside the wire being careful to not cut the stitching. Pinch the center of the wing unit together so that it measures approximately 1½" (3.8cm) from top to bottom. Stitch this gathered area to the leotard about 1" (2.5cm) below the top center back. (Figure 9)

Figure 8

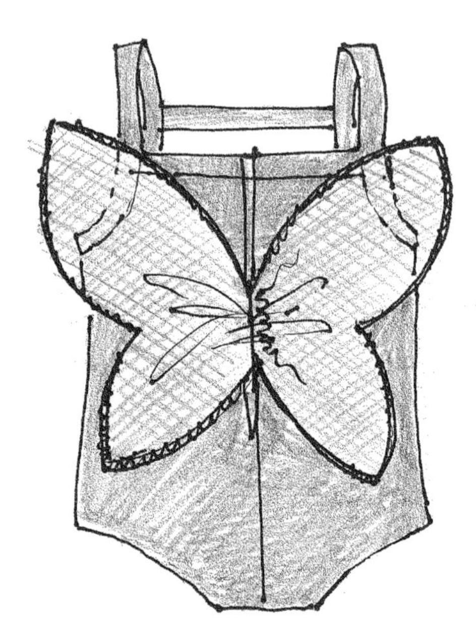

Figure 9

Wreath Instructions

1 Make a circle with the heavy wire, overlapping the ends by ½" (13mm).

2 Beginning at the junction, place a flower or spray on the wire, wrapping the wire stem around the wreath several times. Cut off the excess wire. Wrap the floral tape around the wreath, covering the wire stem. If desired, use bias tape to wrap the stem and use glue to secure the flowers or sprays.

3 Add more flowers or sprays next to the previous one. Wrap the wire stem and then cover with the floral tape. Repeat until the entire wreath is covered with flowers. (Figure 10)

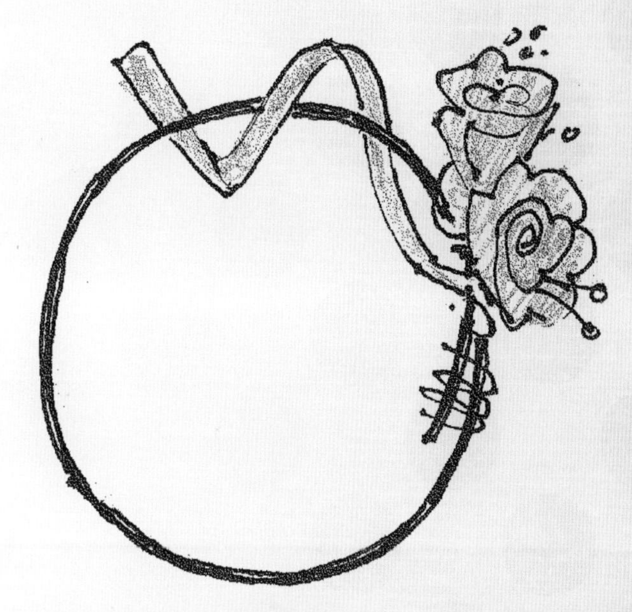

Figure 10

Here's a Hint

The leotard in this outfit can be used to make a swimsuit using the same stretchy knit fabrics. Choose brightly colored prints or solids, add sunglasses and your doll is ready for the beach!

Fun & Fancy

Ballerina

Leotard, Skirt and Slippers

Piroettes are effortless when your doll wears this matching leotard and skirt. The leotard is made just like the one in the *Lilac Fairy* costume. Add your own decorative flowers or trim. Complete with handmade ballet shoes, your doll is sure to get a part in the Nutcracker ballet!

Leotard Supplies:

- *Ballerina* pattern pieces: Leotard Front, Leotard Back
- ¼ yard (0.2m) Lycra knit fabric
- 9½" (24.1cm) elastic, ⅛" (3mm) wide
- ⅔ yard (0.6m) fold-over elastic, ⅝" (16mm) wide
- 4" (10.2cm) strip of hook and loop tape, cut in half lengthwise
- 1 ribbon rose, ½" (13mm) wide

Skirt Supplies:

- 2½" × 16" (6.4cm × 40.6cm) satin fabric
- 10½" (26.7cm) elastic strip, ¼" (6mm) wide
- 3 pieces of 4" × 58" (10.2cm × 47.3cm) netting

Ballet Slippers Supplies:

- *Ballerina* pattern pieces: Slippers Upper, Slippers Sole
- ¼ yard (0.2m) pink satin
- 1¼ yard (1.1m) pink double-faced satin ribbon, ⅛" (3mm) wide

Leotard Instructions

Follow the instructions for the Leotard in the *Lilac Fairy* costume. Tack a ribbon rose to the center front on the fold-over elastic.

Skirt Instructions

1 Fold the satin piece in half lengthwise, wrong sides together, and serge or zigzag the raw edges together. Stitch ½" (13mm) away from the fold to make a casing. (Figure 1)

2 Place the netting pieces on top of each other. To gather the top edge, take one stitch at the top of the netting and pull up the bobbin thread. Pull the bobbin thread at least two yards long. Lay the bobbin thread along the top edge of the skirt and zigzag over it. (Figure 2)

3 Pull the bobbin thread so that the netting is the same width as the serged edge of the waistband. Place the netting and serged waistband edge right sides together and stitch. (The stitching will be underneath the skirt when finished.)

4 Insert the 10½" (26.7cm) piece of ¼" (6mm) elastic in the casing and secure the ends at each side. Fold the netting down and stitch the center back seam of the waistband with right sides together. (Figure 3)

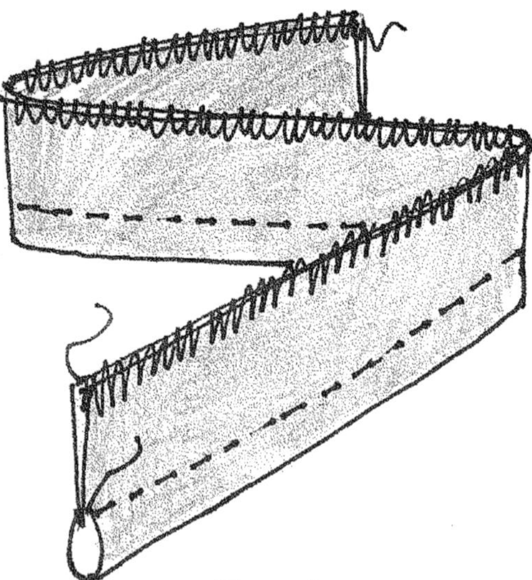

Figure 1

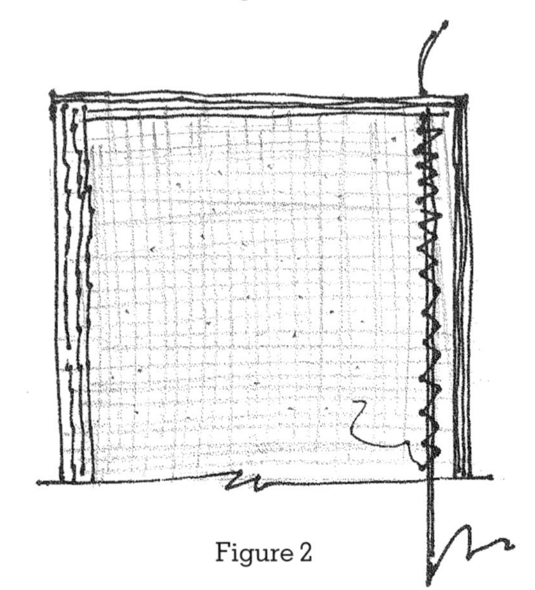

Figure 2

Figure 3

Slippers Instructions

1 From the satin fabric, cut four ballet slipper uppers (you will use two for lining) and two soles.

2 Pin a slipper upper to a lining, right sides together, and stitch around the inside curved edge. (Figure 4) Clip the curves, open and press the seam.

3 With right sides together, stitch the heel seam. Fold the lining down and treat both layers as one unit. (Figure 5)

4 Carefully pin the sole to the upper unit. Straight stitch around the edge. (Figure 6) Finish the seam with a zigzag stitch or by serging.

5 Cut the ribbon in half. Find the center of one piece and stitch it inside the back seam ¼" (6mm) from the top edge of the slipper. Repeat with the second slipper. (Figure 7)

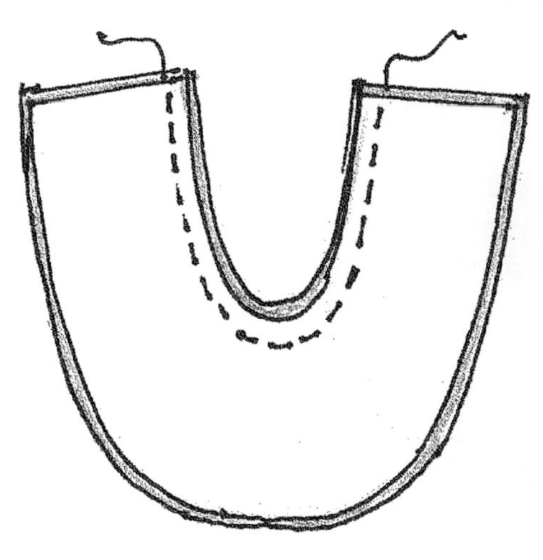

Figure 4

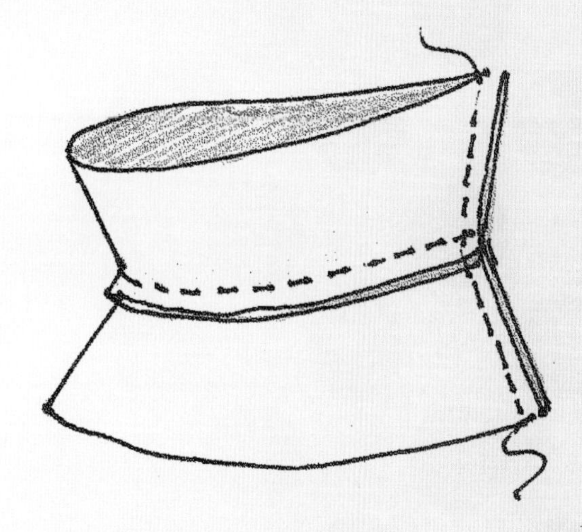

Figure 5

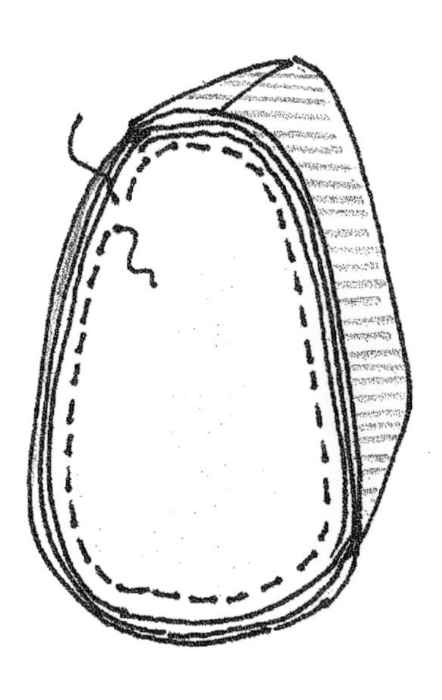

Figure 6

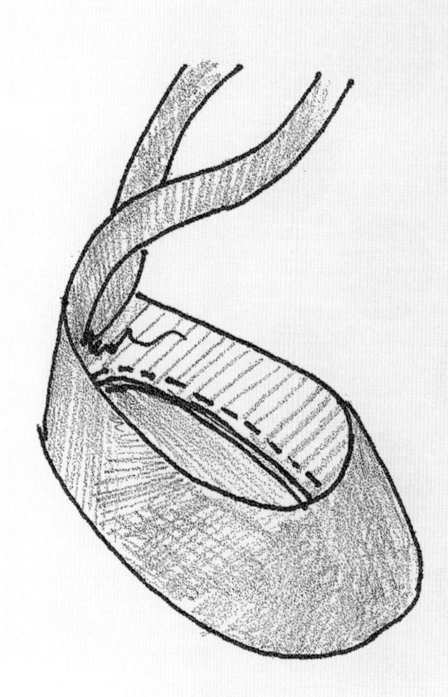

Figure 7

Fun & Fancy

Fairy Tale Wedding Gown

Dress, Veil and Bouquet

Every doll can have a fairy tale wedding with this costume. It is not as complicated as it looks. The gown was made from an eyelet fabric that is embroidered with shiny threads and few holes. The fabric looks like beaded embroidery but is easier to sew on than a shiny or slippery fabric. The hoop skirt gives the gown the fullness it needs. Add lace appliqués found in the bridal section of your local fabric store to the bodice and waistline for the perfect gown.

Dress Supplies

- *Fairy Tale Wedding Gown* pattern pieces: Bodice Front, Bodice Back, Sleeve, Skirt Cutting Guide
- ⅔ yard (0.6m) white eyelet fabric
- 9" (22.9cm) elastic, ⅛" (3mm) wide
- 11" × 19" (27.9cm × 48.3cm) white cotton fabric
- 3 yards (2.7m) pregathered lace, 1¾" (4.4cm) wide
- 3" (7.6cm) strip of hook and loop tape
- 10" (25.4cm) ribbon, ⅛" (3mm) wide
- lace appliqué for bodice, 1" (2.5cm) diameter
- lace appliqué for waistline, 1¼" (3.2cm) diameter

Slip with Hoops Supplies (optional):

- 12¾" × 36" (32.4cm × 91.4cm) rectangle of white broadcloth
- 11½" (29.2cm) elastic, ¼" (6mm) wide
- 2¼ yards (2.1m) of covered plastic boning

Veil Supplies

- *Fairy Tale Wedding Gown* pattern pieces: Tiara, Tiara Base
- 17" × 72" (43.2cm × 182.9cm) piece of netting
- 3 yards (2.7m) narrow lace edging
- 14" (35.6cm) of 18-gauge wire
- 2 yards (1.8m) white satin ribbon, ⅛" (3mm) wide
- scrap of satin fabric
- scrap of lightweight cardboard
- scrap of medium-weight interfacing
- ¼ yard (0.2m) lace trim with scalloped pearl edge, ⅝" (16mm) wide
- 3 glue-on flowers, ⅝" (16mm) wide
- 1 package of pearl stickers, 5mm (packaged with pearls in a row)
- fabric glue

Bouquet Supplies

- 3 clusters of satin flowers with leaves*
- 2 yards (1.8m) satin ribbon, ¼" (6mm) wide
- 1½ yards (1.4m) satin ribbon, ⅛" (3mm) wide
- fabric glue

**Find the flowers for this easy bridal bouquet in the bridal section of fabric and craft stores. Sometimes called "picks," they are a group of flowers and leaves with wire stems about 3"–4" (8cm–10cm) long. The stems are wrapped together with paper. Fan the leaves out around the flowers for a classic look.*

Dress Instructions

1 Cut two bodice fronts, four bodice backs and two sleeves from eyelet fabric. Cut an 11" × 45" (27.9cm × 114.3cm) skirt from the eyelet fabric.

2 With right sides together, sew the shoulder seams of one front and two backs. Press seam allowances open. Repeat with remaining pieces for the lining.

3 With right sides together, pin the lining to the bodice. Stitch up one center back, around the neckline and down the other center back. (Figure 1) Clip the curves and corners. Turn to the right side and press.

4 Press the lower edges of the sleeves ¼" (6mm) to the wrong side. Press under another ¼" (6mm) and stitch to create a casing. Cut the piece of 9" (22.9cm) elastic in half and insert each piece into a sleeve casing. Stitch at the ends to secure. (Figure 2)

5 Gather the sleeve caps between marks. With right sides together, sew the sleeve caps to the armholes. Sew the underarm seams and press. (Figure 3)

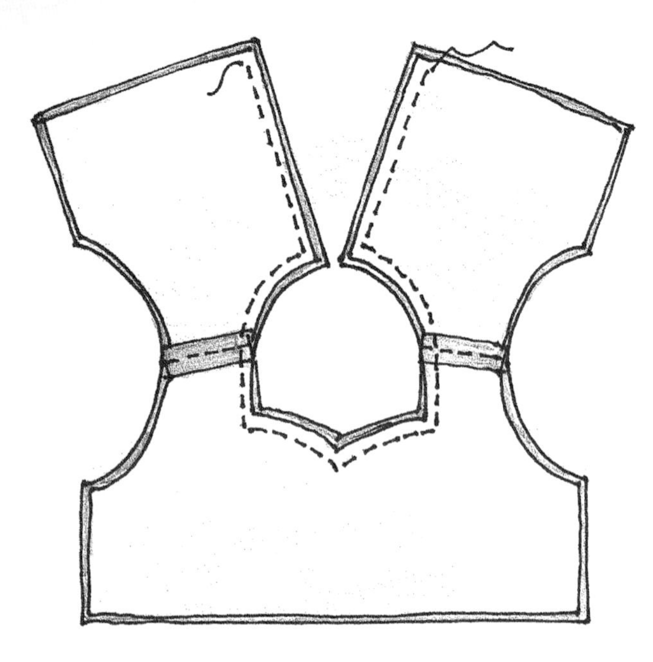

Figure 1

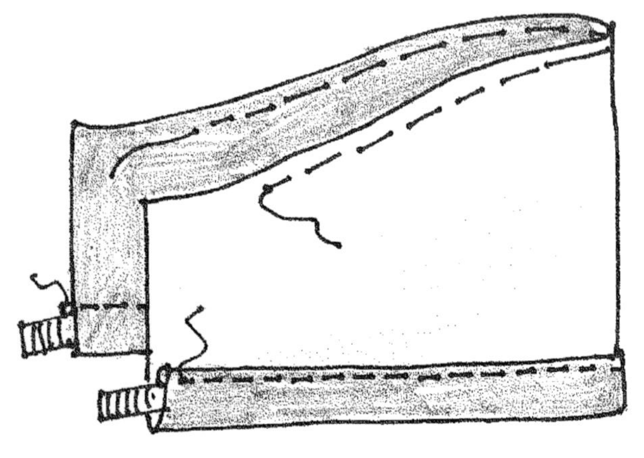

Figure 2

Figure 3

6 To make the skirt, cut the skirt piece into two sections. One should measure 11" × 21" (27.9cm × 53.3cm) and the other 11" × 24" (27.9cm × 61cm). Use the skirt cutting guide pattern piece to round the corners that will be placed in the front. Serge or zigzag stitch the curved front and lower edge and the straight 11" (27.9cm) side of each piece. Press these edges ¼" (6mm) to the wrong side and stitch in place. (Figure 4)

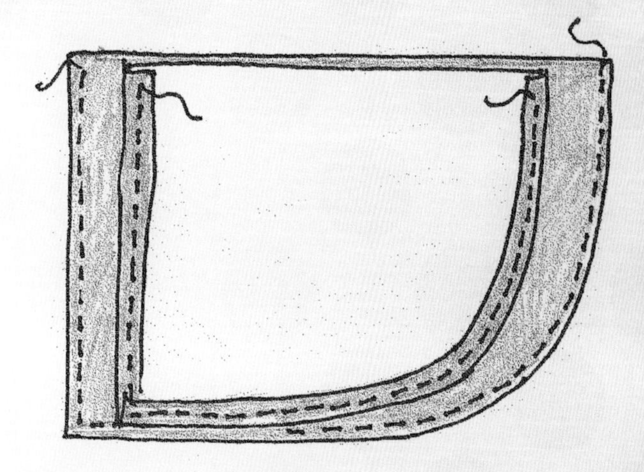

Figure 4

7 Gather the top edge of the skirt pieces. With right sides together, pin and stitch the gathered skirt to the bodice. The 24" (61cm) skirt piece should be pinned to the right half of the bodice and the 21" (53.3cm) piece to the left half. There should be a 1" (2.5cm) gap between the skirts slightly right of the waistband center.

8 To make the skirt insert, serge or zigzag stitch all sides of the white cotton fabric. Press the two 11" (28cm) sides and one 19" (48.3cm) side ¼" (6mm) to the wrong side and stitch in place. Gather the top edge so that it measures 8" (20.3cm) wide. (Figure 5)

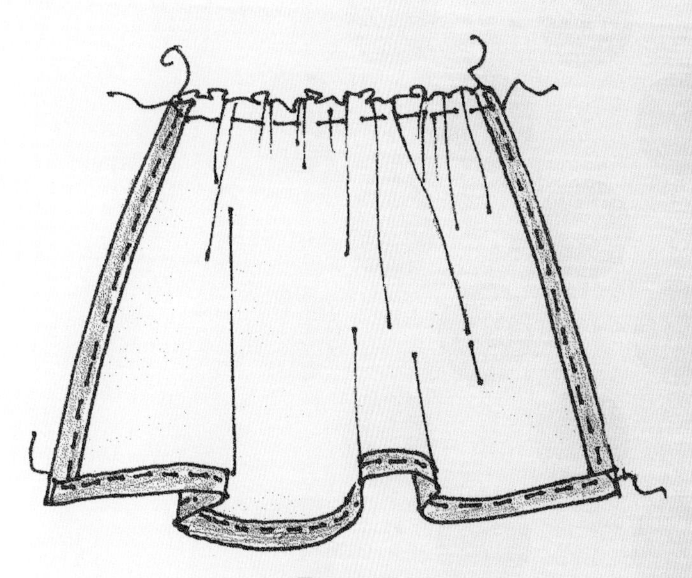

Figure 5

9 Cut the lace into the following pieces: row 1—3" (7.6cm), row 2—5" (12.7cm), row 3—7" (17.8cm), row 4—8" (20.3cm), row 5—11" (27.9cm), row 6—11" (27.9cm), row 7—11" (27.9cm), row 8—14" (35.6cm), and row 9—17" (43cm). Zigzag the 3" (7.6cm) piece in the center of the top gathered edge of the insert. (The lace does not extend to the edges of the insert.) Pin the 5" (12.7cm) piece to the center of the insert just below the first row of lace so that the heading is covered and stitch. Continue down the skirt placing the lace heading just under the previous one, following the order listed above. (Figure 6)

Figure 6

10 Pin and stitch the insert to the waistline, centering the insert over the gap in the skirts. Press the skirt seam allowances toward the bodice. (Figure 7)

11 Lapping right over left, sew hook and loop tape to the back opening.

12 Tack the smaller lace appliqué to the center of the bodice neckline.

13 Cut the ribbon in half. Make three or four loops with each piece and stitch together in a cluster. Tack the larger lace appliqué to the waistline at the gap in the skirts, placing the ribbon loops underneath the sides of the appliqué. (Figure 8)

Figure 7

Slip with Hoops Instructions

Refer to the *Useful Accessories* section for detailed instructions.

Bouquet Instructions

1 Put the stems of the three clusters together. Glue one end of the ¼" (6mm) ribbon directly under the flowers. Wrap the ribbon tightly around the stems from top to bottom. Glue the end and cut off any excess.

2 Cut the ⅛" (3mm) ribbon into four pieces. With all the ribbons together, knot the ribbons at the base of the flowers.

Figure 8

Photo: Bouquet

Veil Instructions

1 Round off the two lower corners of the netting. Sew lace to the sides and curved lower edge of the netting. (Figure 9)

2 Form a circle with the wire, overlapping the ends by ½" (13mm). Wrap the ribbon around the wire to cover, and tack at the ends to secure.

3 Take one stitch at the top edge of the veil. Pull up the bobbin thread and pull it at least 2 yards (1.8m) long. Lay the bobbin thread along the top edge of the veil, and stitch over the bobbin thread with a narrow zigzag stitch. Pull the bobbin thread so that the top of the veil gathers until it measures 6" (15.2cm) wide. Hand stitch the netting to the back edge of the wire. (Figure 10)

4 Cut one bridal tiara from the satin fabric. Cut one bridal tiara base from the cardboard and one from the interfacing. Center the cardboard tiara on the wrong side of the satin tiara. Fold and glue the edges of the satin tiara around the edge of the wire and the back of the cardboard. (Figure 11)

5 Glue scalloped trim to the top edge of the tiara. Stick pearls along the lower edge of the tiara. Glue three flowers to the center of the tiara approximately ½" (13mm) apart. Glue one pearl between each flower. Glue three more pearls on either side of the row of flowers. (Figure 12)

6 Glue the interfacing to the wrong side of the tiara to cover the raw edges of the satin.

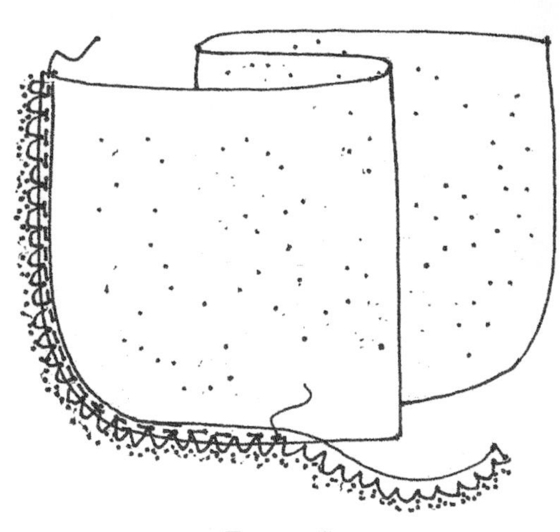

Figure 9

Figure 10

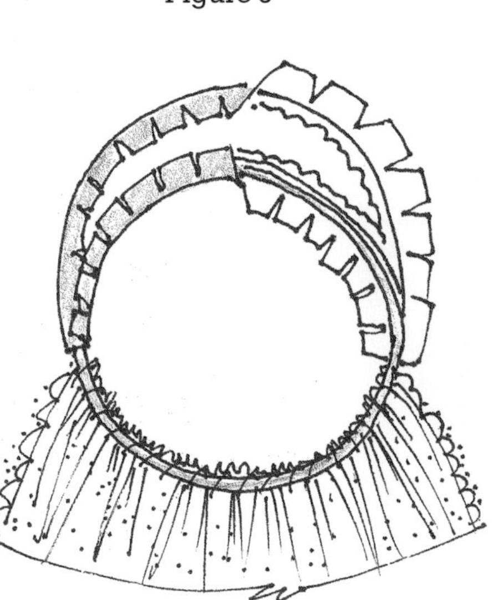

Figure 11

Figure 12

Fun & Fancy

Cinderella

Dress and Glass Slippers

Be the fairy godmother for your doll when you make this lavish ball gown. In this variation of the *Fairy Tale Wedding Gown*, the dress is made from satin with sequin and rhinestone trims. The layers of lace are eliminated from the skirt insert and replaced with a sheer overlay of blue hearts. The most important part—the "glass slippers"—are made from a clear vinyl found in fabric stores. If you can't find a flexible medium-weight vinyl, look for a clear vinyl bag in office supply or discount stores. Add a glittery tiara found in craft or party stores for the finishing touch.

Dress Supplies

Cinderella pattern pieces: Bodice Front, Bodice Back, Sleeve, Skirt Cutting Guide

⅔ yard (0.6m) satin fabric

9" (22.8cm) elastic, ⅛" (3mm) wide

½ yard (0.5m) rhinestone trim, ⅜" (10mm) wide

1 teardrop pearl bead, ⅝" (16mm) long

11" × 18" (27.9cm × 45.9cm) piece of white cotton fabric

4 yards (3.7m) sequin trim, ½" (13mm) wide

11" × 18" (27.9cm × 45.9cm) piece of sheer overlay fabric

½ yard (0.5m) lace edging, 1½" (3.8cm) wide

3" (7.6cm) strip of hook and loop tape

1 ribbon rose, size 1"–1½" (2.5cm–3.8cm)

Slip with Hoops Supplies (optional):

12¾" × 36" (32.4cm × 91.4cm) rectangle of white broadcloth

11½" (29.2cm) elastic, ¼" (6mm) wide

2¼ yards (2.1m) of covered plastic boning

Glass Slippers Supplies

Cinderella pattern pieces: Glass Slippers Upper, Glass Slippers Sole

9" × 12" (22.8cm × 30.5cm) craft foam sheet with adhesive back

9" × 12" (22.8cm × 30.5cm) clear vinyl, medium weight

fabric glue

14" (35.6cm) pearl trim, ⅛" (3mm) wide

2 ribbon roses, size ½" (13mm)

Dress Instructions

1 Cut two bodice fronts, four bodice backs, two sleeves and an 11" × 45" (27.9cm × 114.3cm) skirt piece from the satin fabric.

2 Follow steps 2–5 for the *Fairy Tale Wedding Gown*.

3 Hand stitch the rhinestone trim to the bodice. Sew the pearl bead at the center front. (Figure 1)

4 To make the skirt, cut the skirt piece into two sections. One section should measure 11" × 21" (27.9cm × 53.3cm) and the other 11" × 24" (27.9cm × 61cm). The longer piece will be stitched to the left side of the bodice and the shorter one to the right side. Use the skirt cutting guide pattern piece to round the corners that will be placed in the front. (Figure 2) Serge or zigzag stitch the curved front and lower edges and the straight 11" (27.9cm) side of each piece. Press them ¼" (6mm) to the wrong side, and stitch the short ends.

5 Stitch the sequin trim over the curved front and lower edges. Fold the ends of the trim under each center back edge.

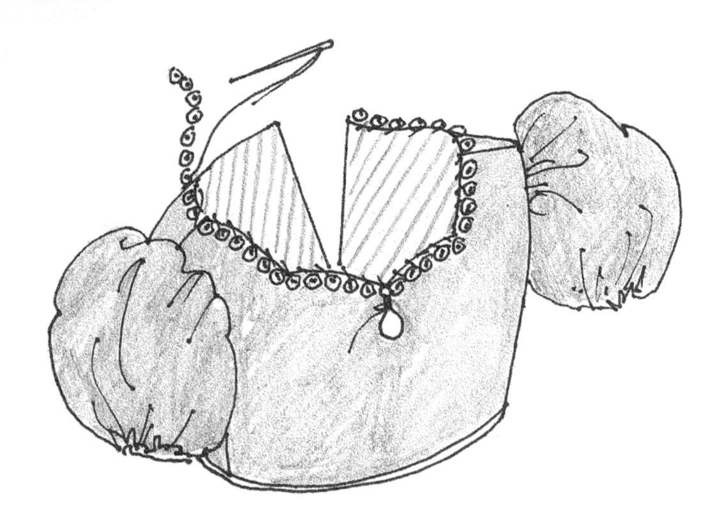

Figure 1

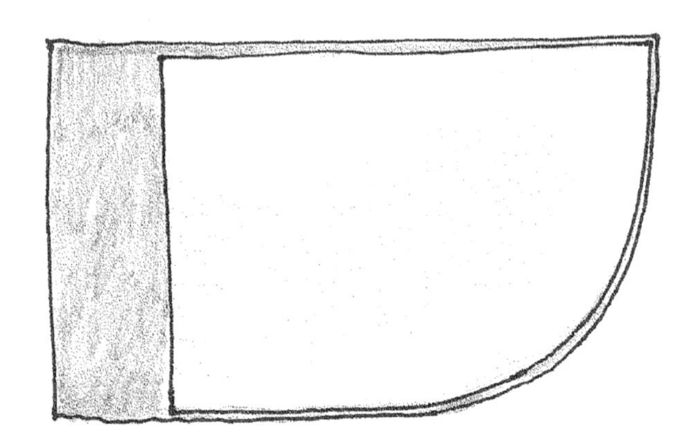

Figure 2

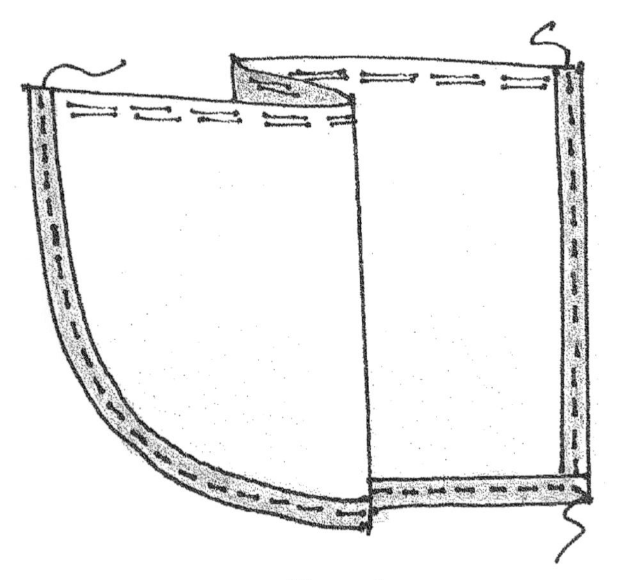

Figure 3

6 Gather the top edge of the skirts. (Figure 3) With right sides together, pin and stitch them to the bodice. (Figure 4)

7 To create the insert, place the sheer fabric over the white fabric. (From now on, treat the fabrics of the insert as one.) Serge or zigzag stitch all sides of the skirt insert. Press the two 11" (27.9cm) sides and one 18" (45.7cm) side of the insert ¼" (6mm) to the wrong side and stitch. Place the wide lace edging along the pressed lower edge and stitch in place. (Figure 5) Gather the top edge so that it measures 8" (20.3cm) wide.

8 Pin the insert to the waistline, centering it over the gap in the skirts, and stitch. Press the skirt seam allowances toward the bodice. (Figure 6)

9 Lapping right over left, sew the hook and loop tape to the back opening.

10 Tack the ribbon rose to the gap in the skirts at the waistline.

Slip with Hoops Instructions

Refer to the *Useful Accessories* section for detailed instructions.

Figure 4

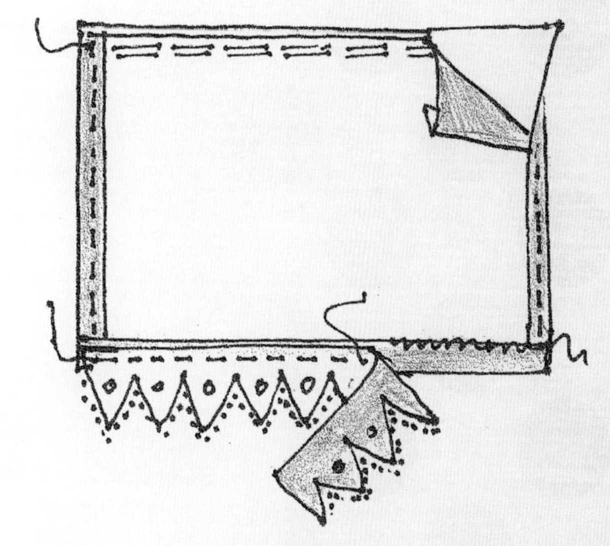

Figure 5

Figure 6

Glass Slippers Instructions

1 Cut four soles from the craft foam. Cut two shoe uppers from the vinyl.

2 Overlap the back edge of each upper by ¼" (6mm) and glue. (Figure 7) Clip the outer edges of the vinyl about ¼" (6mm).

3 Peel the paper off one of the soles. Beginning at the center front, fold the clipped edge of the vinyl over the edge of the sole, adhering the vinyl to the adhesive back. Continue around the shoe until the entire slashed edge is pressed over the sole.

4 Peel the paper off another sole and glue to the underside of the shoe. The clipped vinyl edge will be sandwiched in between the soles. Repeat with the remaining upper and soles. (Figure 8)

5 Glue the pearl trim along the upper edge of the shoes. Glue a ribbon rose to the center of the shoe. (Figure 9)

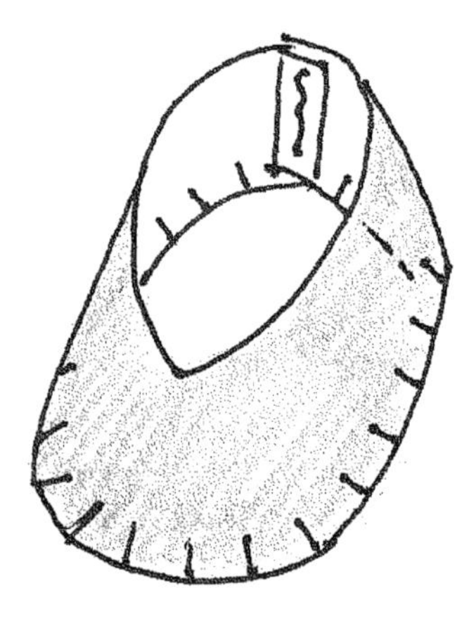

Figure 7

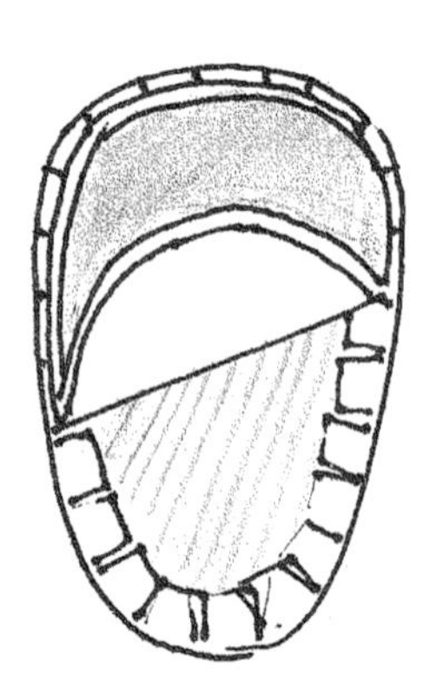

Figure 8

Figure 9

Here's a Hint

Girls love all fairy-tale princesses in beautiful ball gowns. This dress is easily adaptable to other stories.

For Rapunzel, make a band of matching fabric to go around the doll's head. Attach a long braid at one side made from yarn that matches the doll's hair.

For Snow White, add a headband with a large bow at the front. The skirt can be simplified by eliminating the insert. Keep the skirt all one piece and stitch it to the bodice. It can be trimmed with rows of glittery ribbon trim or sequins.

To make yet another skirt variation, create an underskirt and attach it to the waistline with the top skirt. Pinch the bottom of the top skirt up about 2" (5cm) at 5"–6" (12.7cm–15.2cm) intervals around the bottom edge. Cover the pinched spots with bows or large ribbon roses.

Let your imagination run wild! With this costume as your base garment, you can create any fairy-tale garment you can dream up.

Fun & Fancy

Southern Belle

Dress, Hat and Slip with Hoops

If you listen carefully, you can hear your doll saying "Fiddle-dee-dee." This full-skirted dress has a slip with hoops to go underneath to create an authentic Civil War-era costume. Look for a small leafy green calico for just the right look.

Dress Supplies

Southern Belle pattern pieces: Front, Back

½ yard (0.5m) green and white printed cotton fabric

2½ yards (2.3m) cotton lace edging with gathering thread **or** 32" (81.2cm) pre-gathered lace, 1" (3cm) wide

⅔ yard (0.6m) green velveteen ribbon, ¼" (6mm) wide

1 yard (0.9m) green velveteen ribbon, ⅝" (16mm) wide

3 snaps

Hat Supplies

straw hat with wide brim

⅔ yard (0.6m) ribbon, ⅝" (16mm) wide

Slip with Hoops Supplies

12¾" × 36" (32.4cm × 91.4cm) rectangle of white broadcloth

11½" (29.2cm) elastic, ¼" (6mm) wide

2¼ yards (2.1m) of covered plastic boning

Dress Instructions

1 Cut out two fronts and four backs from the printed cotton fabric. Cut a 12" × 40" (30.4cm × 101.6cm) skirt.

2 Sew the shoulder seams together with one front and two backs. Repeat with the remaining pieces for the lining. Press seam allowances open. (Figure 1)

3 With right sides together, stitch up one of the center backs, around the neckline and down the other center back. Stitch around each armhole. (Figure 2) Clip curves and turn to right side. Press.

4 Cut one yard of lace. Pull the gathering thread in the heading to gather. Turn each end under. Hand stitch the lace heading ½" (13mm) away from the neckline seam. (If using pregathered lace, cut 13" [33cm] and hand stitch, tucking in the ends.) Cut another yard of lace and gather. Hand stitch the lace heading ¼" (6mm) away from the neckline seam. (If using pregathered lace, cut 13" [33cm] and stitch as above.) Cut the remaining lace in half. Gather each piece so that each measures 2" (5cm) long. Place each piece of lace along the top curve of a shoulder seam, using the armhole seam to help center it. Tuck in the ends and stitch in place. (If using pregathered lace, cut the lace into 3" [7.6cm] sections and hand stitch, tucking in the ends.) (Figure 3)

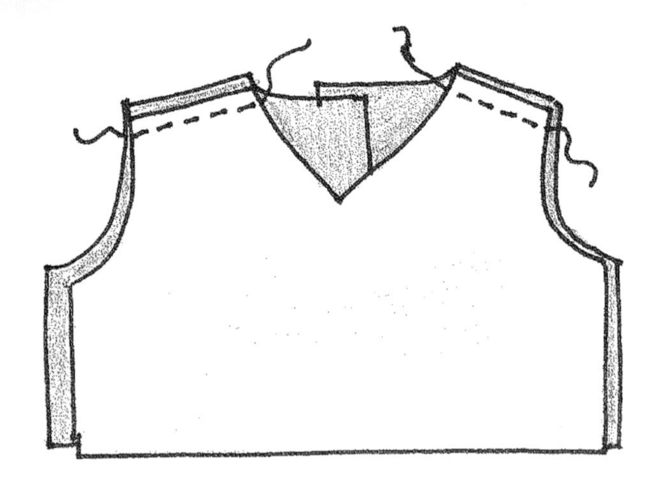

Figure 1

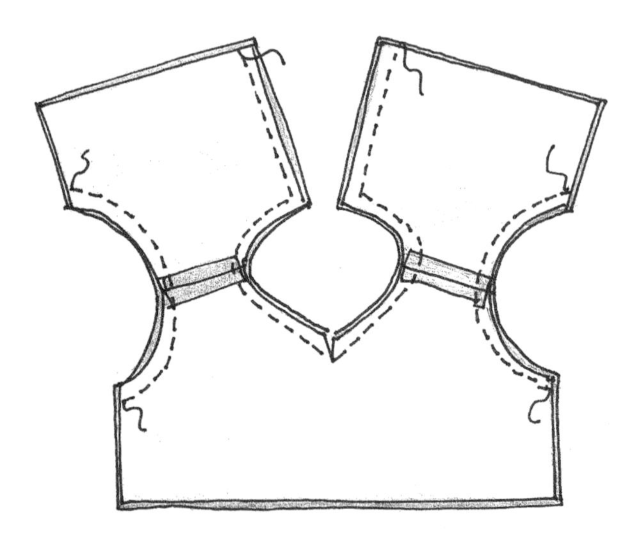

Figure 2

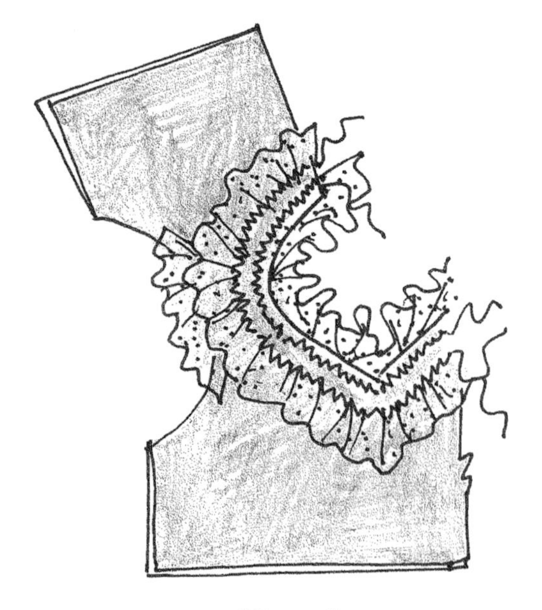

Figure 3

5 Place ¼" (6mm) ribbon over the lace heading on the top row. Tuck the ends under at the center back and hand stitch along the lower edge of the ribbon, easing the ribbon as necessary. Cut the ribbon at the other center back and tuck the end under. Stitch along the top edge of the ribbon. Cut a 12" (30.5cm) piece of narrow ribbon and tie into a bow. Tack the bow to the center front along the ribbon edge. (Figure 4)

6 Sew the underarm seam. (Figure 5)

7 Press the lower edge ½" (13mm) to the wrong side. Press under another ½" (13mm) and stitch in place.

8 With right sides together, sew the center back seam of the skirt, stopping 3" (7.6cm) from the top edge. (Figure 6) Press seam allowances open, including the unstitched part. Topstitch around the opening.

9 Gather the top edge of the skirt. With right sides together, sew the skirt to the bodice. Press the seam allowances toward the bodice. (Figure 7)

10 Cut one yard (0.9mm) of velveteen ribbon. Tie the ribbon around the waist as a sash. Hand tack it at the side seams if desired.

11 Cut the ribbon for the hat ties in half. Stitch one end of one piece to the inside of the brim of the hat. Sew the end of the other piece directly opposite the first ribbon.

Slips with Hoops Instructions

Refer to the *Useful Accessories* section for detailed instructions.

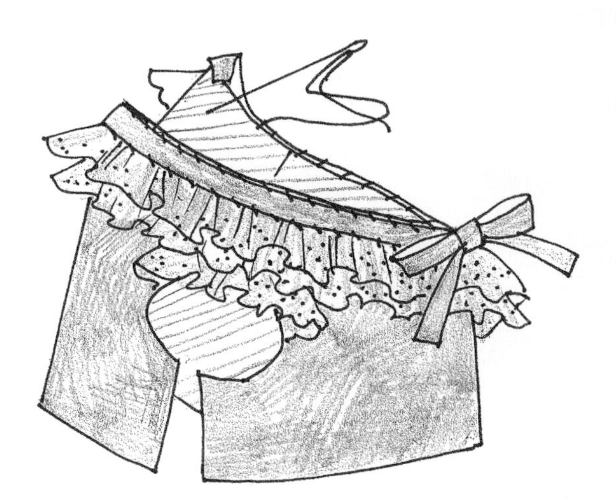

Figure 4

Figure 5

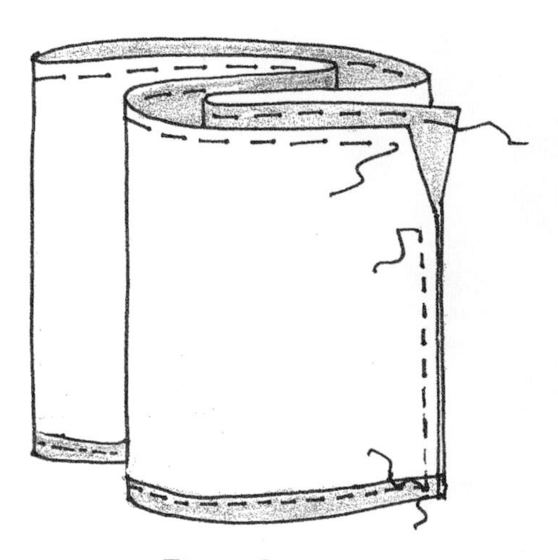

Figure 6

Figure 7

Fun & Fancy

Little Bo Peep

Pantalets, Dress, Staff and Bonnet

This sweet costume is just right for this beloved nursery rhyme. The dress has ribbon lacing on the front which is edged by lace trim. The gathered peplums on the skirt are made from contrasting fabric. Pantalets, also edged with lace, are worn under the dress. The doll has a staff made from bias tape and drinking straws. Add a bonnet and a lamb, and your doll's outfit is complete. This outfit can also be adapted to create a costume from the colonial period. Just extend the skirt to the floor and add the straight ruffled sleeve from the *Witch* costume for an authentic look.

Pantalets and Dress Supplies

- *Little Bo Peep* pattern pieces: Pantalets, Bodice Front, Bodice Back, Bodice Inset, Dress Sleeve, Peplum Cutting Guide
- 10½" (26.7cm) elastic, ¼" (6mm) wide (pantalets)
- ¼ yard (0.2m) cotton print fabric
- ⅔ yard (0.6m) solid cotton fabric
- ⅓ yard (0.3m) white fabric
- 24" (61cm) ribbon, ¼" (6mm) wide
- 2 yards (1.8m) lace edging, ⅝" (16mm) wide
- 8" (20.3cm) elastic, ⅛" (3mm) wide (sleeves)
- 12" (30.5cm) flat eyelet lace, 5" (12.7cm) wide
- 3 snaps or 3" (7.6cm) strip of hook and loop tape, cut in half

Staff and Bonnet Supplies

- 2 flexible drinking straws
- 3"–4" (7.6cm–10.2cm) florist's wire
- 1 package of white single-fold bias tape
- fabric glue
- 1 yard (0.9m) ribbon, ⅞" (22mm) wide
- purchased bonnet

Pantalets Instructions

1 Cut four pantalets from the white fabric.

2 With right sides together, sew the center front and center back seams. (Figure 1) Sew the side seams. (Figure 2)

3 Press the waistline edge ¼" (6mm) to the wrong side. Press another ½" (13mm) to the wrong side. Stitch along the pressed edge to form a casing, leaving a 1" (2.5cm) opening at the back.

4 Thread ¼" (6mm) elastic through the casing and secure the ends. Sew the opening closed.

5 Press the lower edge of the pantalets ¼" (6mm) to the wrong side. Place the heading of the lace under the pressed edge and topstitch. (Figure 3)

6 With right sides together, sew the inner leg seam. (Figure 4)

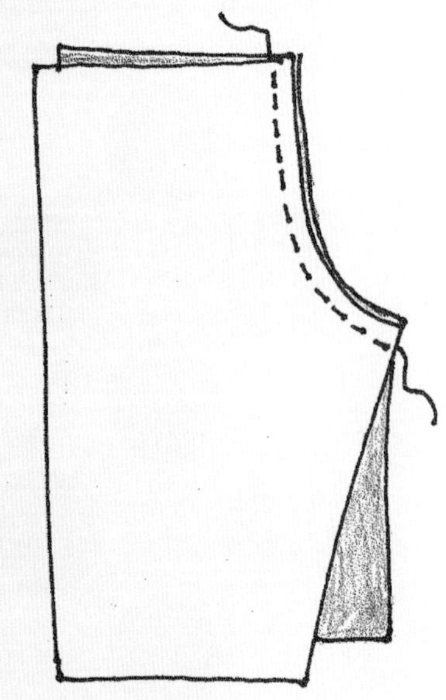

Figure 1

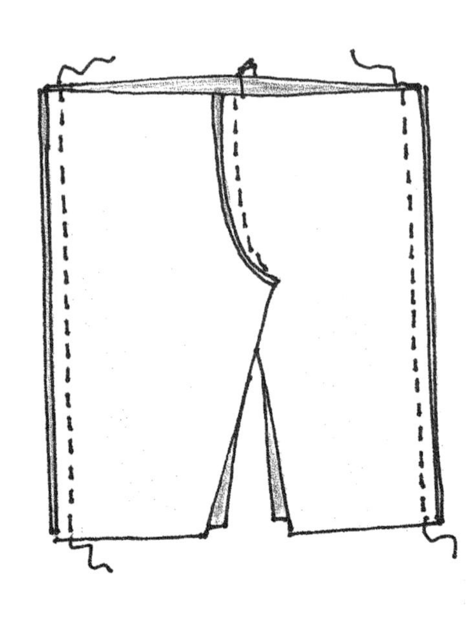

Figure 2

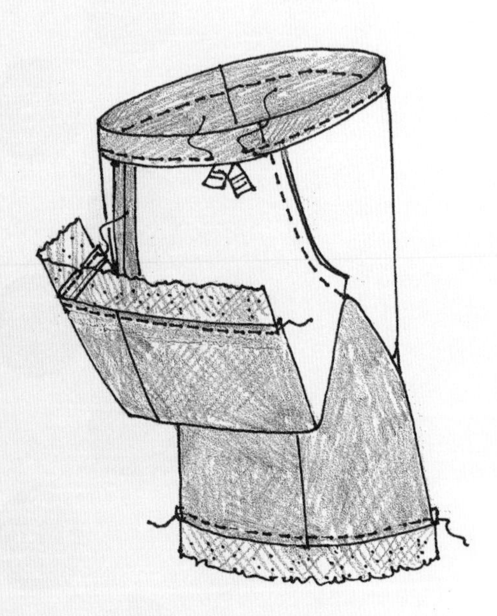

Figure 3

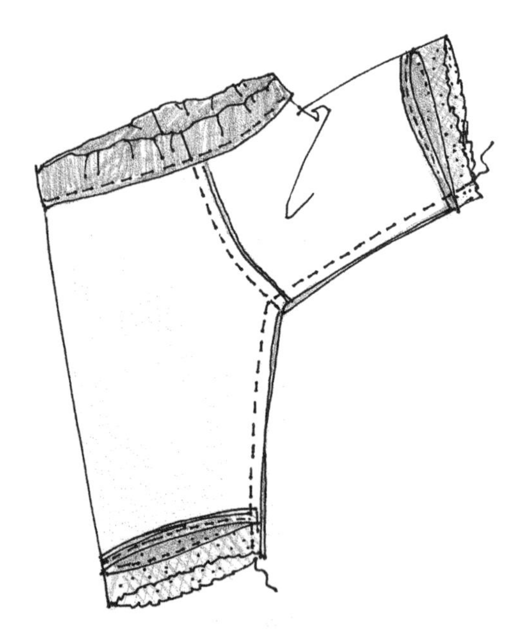

Figure 4

Dress Instructions

1 Cut four bodice fronts and four bodice backs from the solid cotton fabric. Cut two 13" × 21" (33cm × 53.3cm) peplum pieces from the solid cotton fabric. Cut two bodice insets and two sleeves from the white fabric. Cut an 8" × 45" (20.3cm × 114.3cm) skirt from the print cotton fabric.

2 With right sides together, sew a right and left bodice front to a right and left bodice back at the shoulder. Press seam allowances open. Repeat with remaining bodice pieces for the lining. (Figure 5)

3 With right sides together, pin the left bodice (including the front and the back) to the left bodice lining. Repeat with the right bodice and lining. Stitch up the center backs, around the neckline and front of each half. (Figure 6) Clip the curves, turn to the right side and press.

4 With right sides together, sew the bodice insets along the side and top edges. (Figure 7) Leave the bottom edge open, turn to the right side and press.

5 Pin the narrow ribbon at the top marks on the sides of the pattern piece and follow the arrows to create a lacing effect. Stitch along each side of the ribbon to secure. (Figure 8)

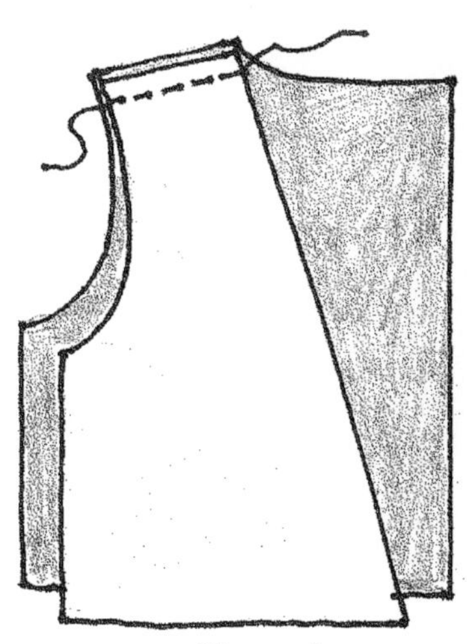

Figure 5

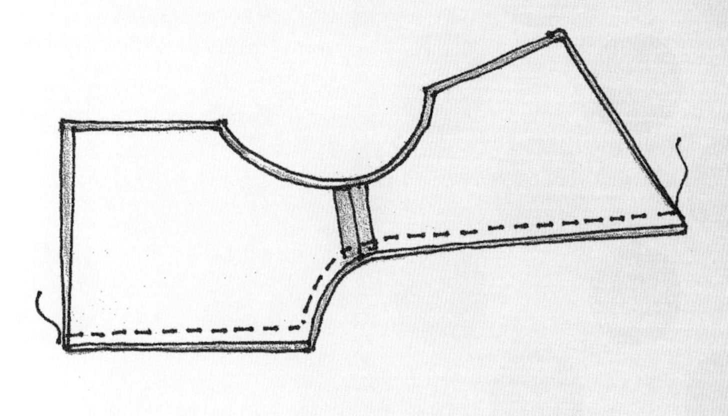

Figure 6

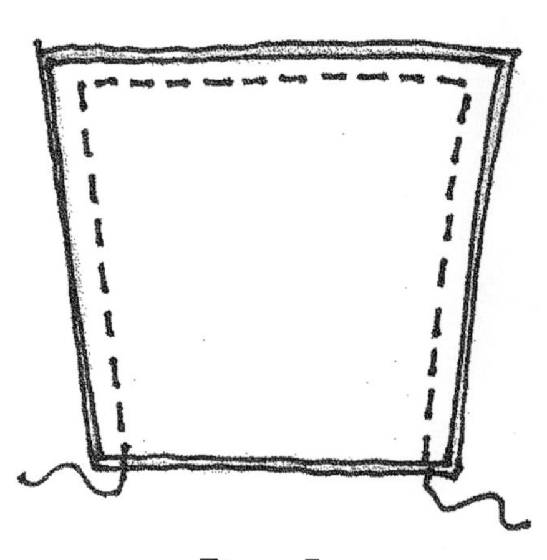

Figure 7

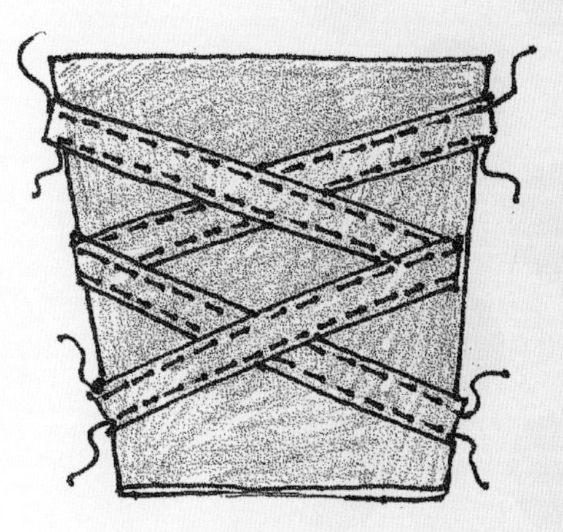

Figure 8

6 Pin the bodice inset in place underneath the bodice right and left front side edges, aligning the lower edge of the inset with the lower edges of the bodice. The top of the inset should be placed ¼" (6mm) under each side of the bodice. The width of the bodice inset at the waistline is about 1" (2.5cm). Baste in place. (Figure 9)

7 Gather two 15" (38.1cm) pieces of ⅝" (16mm) lace edging so that each piece will fit along the back neckline and down each front. Zigzag the lace to the bodice over the basting, turning the end of the lace under ¼" (6mm). Place the remainder of the ribbon over the gathered lace and stitch along both sides, turning in the ends of the ribbon ¼" (6mm) to the wrong side at the back. (Figure 10)

8 Press the lower edge of each sleeve ¼" (6mm) to the wrong side. Using the remainder of the ⅝" (16mm) lace, place the lace heading under the pressed edge and stitch in place. Cut the ⅛" (3mm) elastic in half. Anchor the elastic at one side of the sleeve ¼" (6mm) above the lace edge. Zigzag over the elastic strip, stretching the elastic as you stitch. Be sure not to catch the elastic in the zigzag stitching. Anchor the elastic at the other side of the sleeve. (Figure 11)

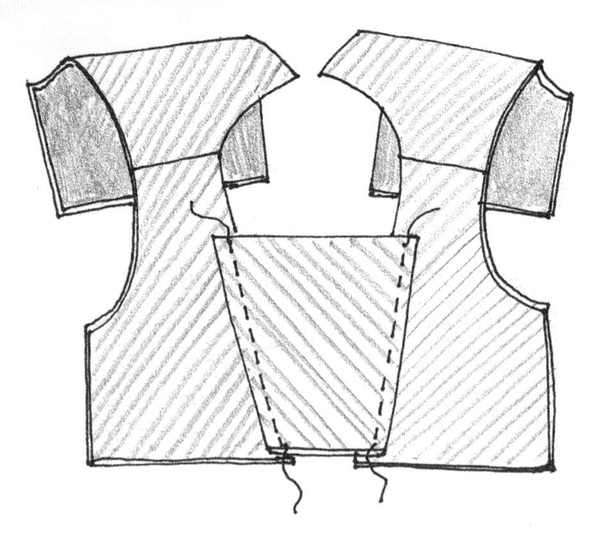

Figure 9

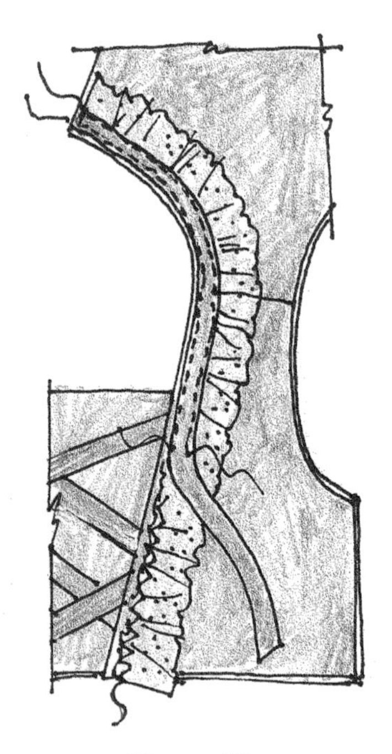

Figure 10

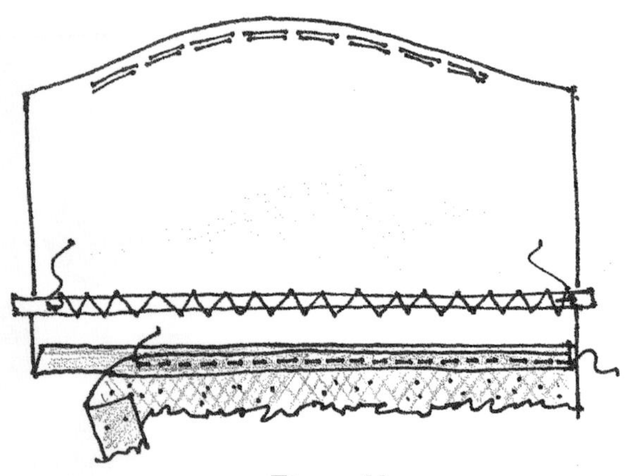

Figure 11

9 Gather the sleeve caps between the marks and stitch the sleeves to each armhole. Sew the underarm seam. (Figure 12)

10 With right sides together, sew the centerback seam of the skirt, stopping 3" (7.6cm) from one edge. Press the seam open and topstitch the opening.

11 On the closed bottom edge, press under ¼" (6mm) to the wrong side. Press up another ¼" (6mm) and stitch.

12 Gather the top edge of the skirt to fit the bodice. (Figure 13)

13 Press the side edges of the eyelet ¼" (6mm) to the wrong side. Press under another ¼" (6mm) and stitch in place. Gather the top edge so that it measures 7" (17.8cm) across. (Figure 14) Pin the top edge of the eyelet to the center right side of the gathered skirt.

Figure 12

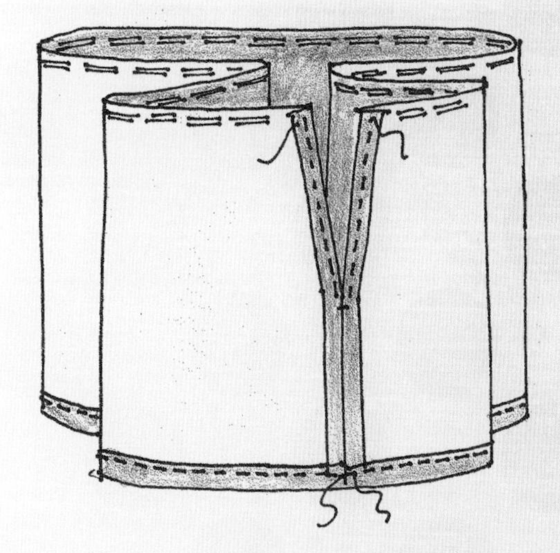

Figure 13

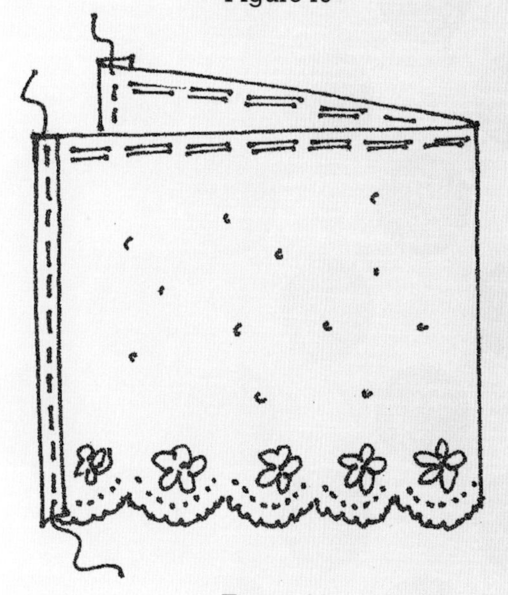

Figure 14

14 With wrong sides together, fold each peplum into quarters, first widthwise, then lengthwise. Use the peplum guide to cut away the corners of the raw edges. Unfold the lengthwise fold (peplum is now folded in half once) and gather the curved edges of each peplum. (Figure 15)

15 Pull the gathering threads so each peplum fits along one-half of the skirt's waistline, with the peplum's front edge aligning with each bodice and inset seam. There will be a 1" (2.5cm) gap for the eyelet apron to show in the center front. (Figure 16) With right sides together, sew the skirt to the bodice. (Figure 17)

16 Sew snaps or hook and loop tape to the back opening.

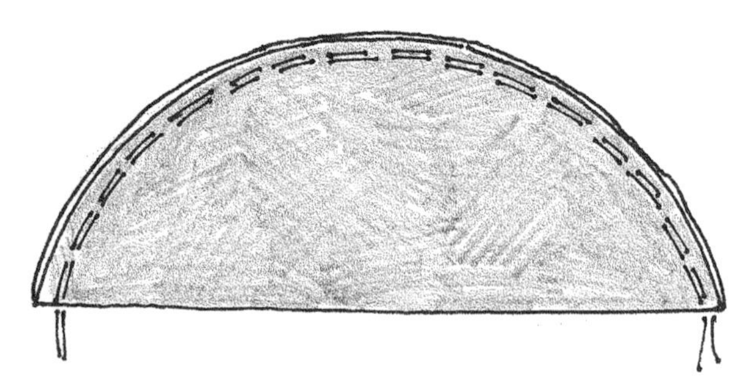

Figure 15

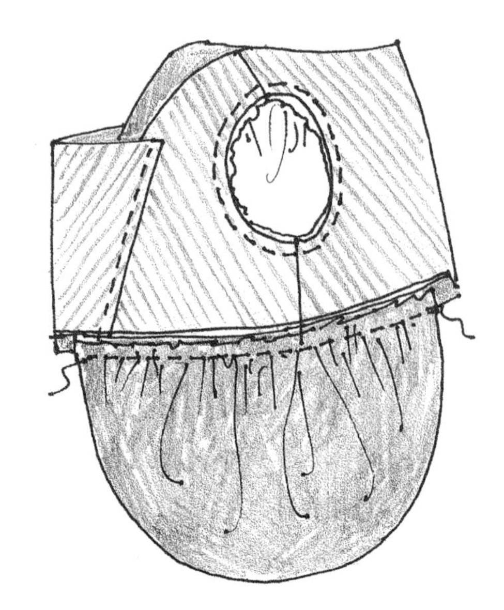

Figure 16

Figure 17

Staff and Bonnet Instructions

1 Cut one straw 5" (12.7cm) from the bottom. Pinch the bottom end of the other straw so that it will fit down into the cut end of the first straw. Place a small dab of glue on the pinched end, and insert approximately ½" (1.3cm) into the other straw.

2 Place the wire into one end of the straw with a flexible neck. Bend the wire so that the straw curves at the end. Glue into place.

3 Wrap the straws with the bias tape and secure with glue at both ends. Tie a ribbon into a bow around the staff. (Figure 18)

4 Tie a ribbon around a bonnet to hold it to the doll's head. (Figure 19)

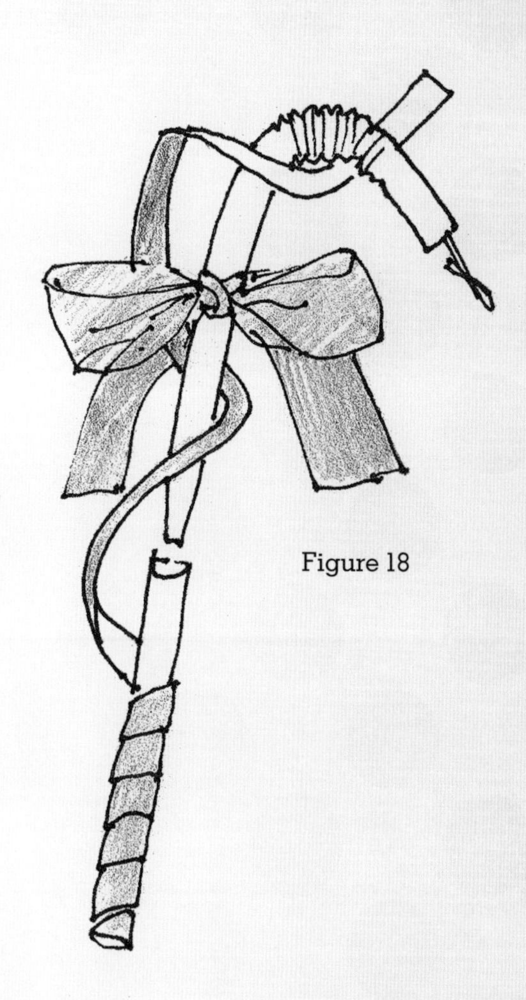

Figure 18

Figure 19

Traditional
Halloween

Witch

Dress and Hat

This pretty little witch costume is sure to become a favorite. The contrasting black and orange prints are perfect for Halloween. The dress has simple trim down the front made by weaving together two pieces of rickrack. Add a bow to the waistline and hat for fun and fashionable accents. This dress style is adaptable for other fairy tale garments such as a poor Cinderella costume. Make it with cream and earth-toned fabrics and eliminate the trim and bow.

Witch Costume Supplies

- *Witch* pattern pieces: Underskirt, Upper Skirt, Dress Front, Dress Back, Dress Sleeve, Dress Sleeve Cuff, Dress Contrasting Front, Hat Crown, Hat Brim
- ½ yard (0.5m) black cotton fabric
- ⅓ yard (0.3m) polka-dot cotton fabric
- 5½" × 3½" (14cm × 8.9cm) of fusible web
- 10" (25.4cm) orange baby rick-rack
- 10" (25.4cm) black baby rick-rack
- monofilament invisible thread
- ¼ yard (0.2m) striped cotton fabric
- 4½" × 12½" (11.4cm × 31.8cm) piece of star print cotton fabric
- 3" (7.6cm) strip of hook and loop tape, cut in half
- ¼ yard (0.2m) heavy-weight interfacing

Dress Instructions

1 Cut two fronts, four backs and two sleeves from the black fabric. Using pinking sheers, cut two cuffs from the polka-dot fabric.

2 Trace the contrasting front onto the paper side of the fusible web. Following the manufacturer's instructions, peel off the paper and press onto the wrong side of the polka-dot fabric. Cut out the contrasting front and fuse to the center of one of the fronts.

3 Cut each piece of rickrack into two 5" (12.7cm) pieces. Weave one orange piece and one black piece together to make a trim. (Figure 1) Place this trim along one side of the contrasting front and zigzag in place with invisible thread. Repeat on the other side. (Figure 2)

4 With right sides together, sew the contrast fabric front to two backs at the shoulders. Press the seam allowances open. Repeat with the remaining pieces for the lining.

5 With right sides together, sew the lining to the bodice up one center back, around the neckline and down the other center back. (Figure 3) Clip the curves, turn right side out and press.

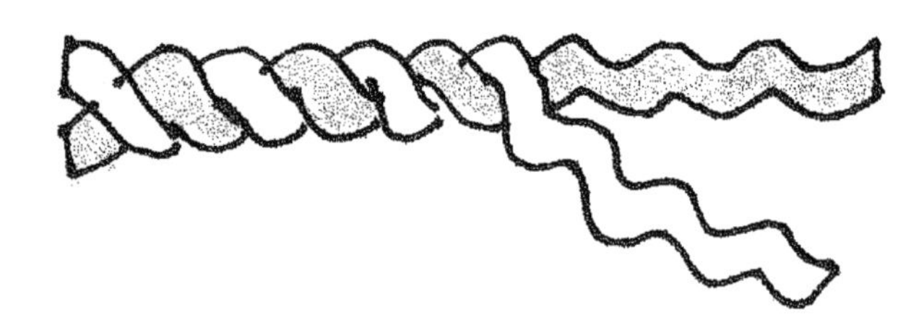

Figure 1

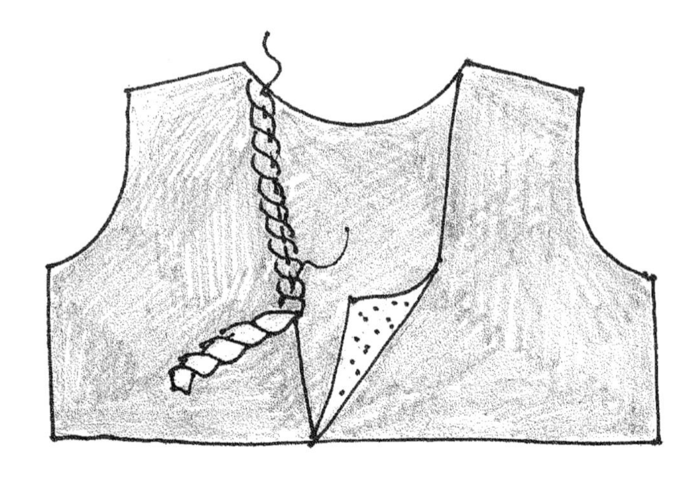

Figure 2

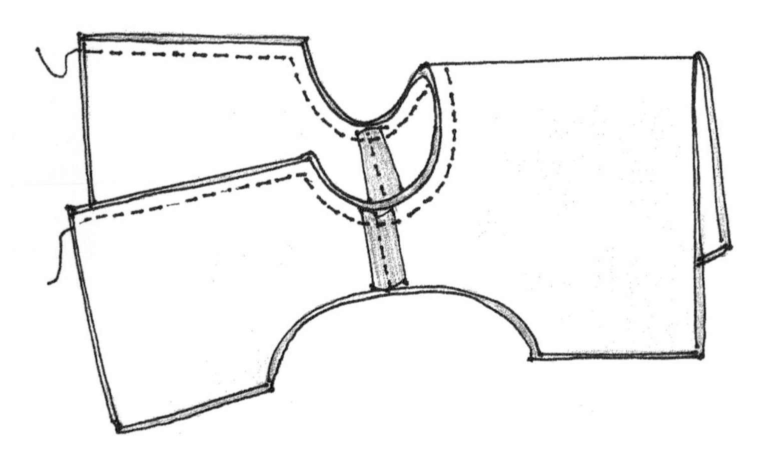

Figure 3

6 With right sides together, sew the cuffs to the lower edge of each sleeve. Press the seam allowances toward the cuff and topstitch on the cuffs close to the seam line. (Figure 4)

7 Sew the sleeves into the armholes with right sides together, easing as necessary. Sew the underarm seam from the cuff edge to the lower edge of the bodice. (Figure 5)

8 Using pinking shears, cut one underskirt from the striped fabric to create the ragged lower edge. Cut an upper skirt from the polka-dot fabric in the same manner.

9 Place the wrong side of the upper skirt to the right side of the underskirt so that the top and side raw edges match. Treating the skirts as one unit, press the side edges ¼" (6mm) to the wrong side and stitch.

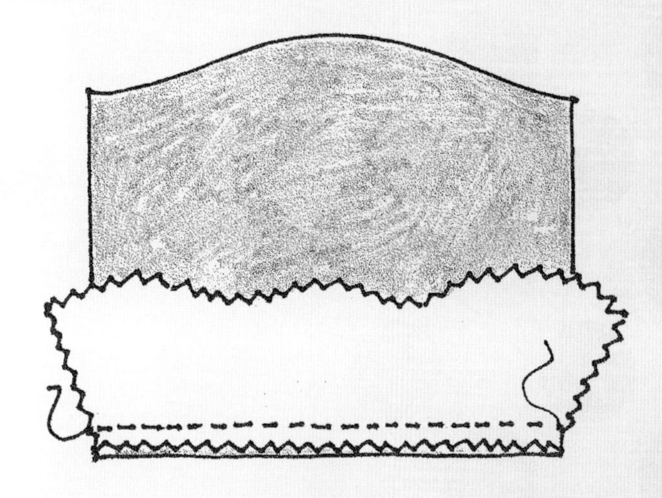

Figure 4

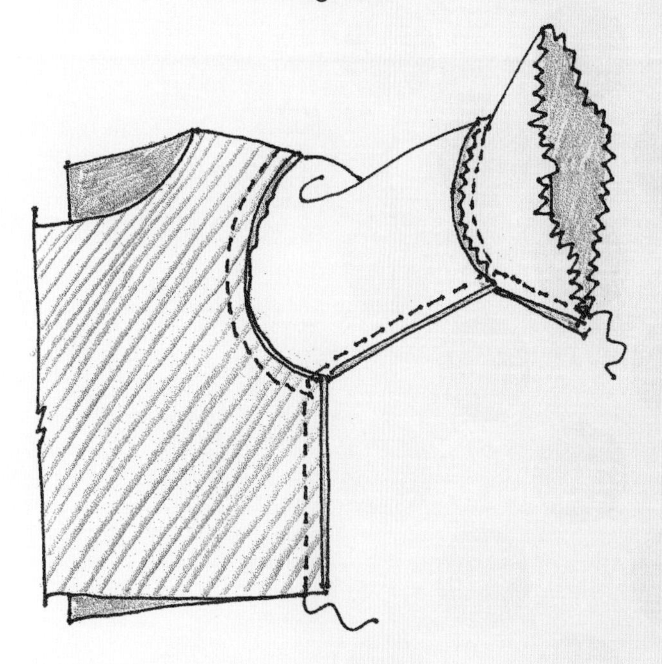

Figure 5

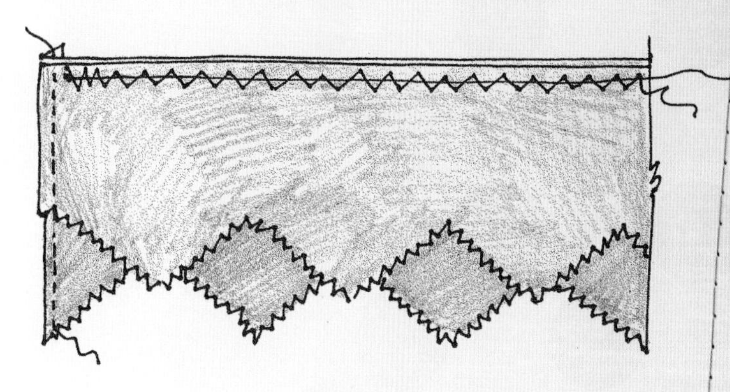

Figure 6

10 To gather the top edge, take one stitch at one side of the skirt and pull up the bobbin thread. Pull the bobbin thread at least as wide as the skirt. Place the thread along the top edge of the skirt. Zigzag over the bobbin thread, being careful not to catch the thread in the stitches. (Figure 6) Pull the bobbin thread to gather the skirt until it is the same width as the bodice. With right sides together, sew the skirt to the bodice. (Figure 7)

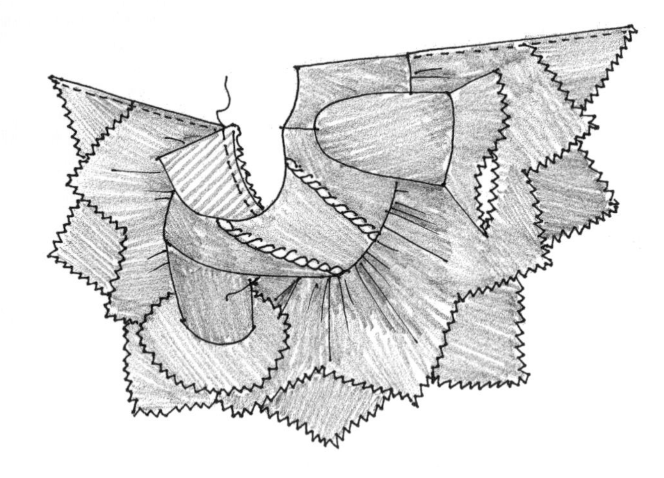

Figure 7

11 To make the bow, cut a 3½" (8.9cm) square and a 1¼" × 2" (3.2cm × 5.1cm) rectangle from the star print fabric. With right sides together, fold the square piece in half and stitch along one end and the long side edge. (Figure 8) Turn to the right side and press. Fold the remaining end ¼" (6mm) to the wrong side and topstitch it closed. Fold the smaller piece in thirds so that it measures ¾" × 1¼" (1.9cm × 3.2cm). Pinch the bow tightly in the center and wrap the folded piece around it. Tack the edges together at the back. (Figure 9) Tack the bow to the waistline at the center of the bodice.

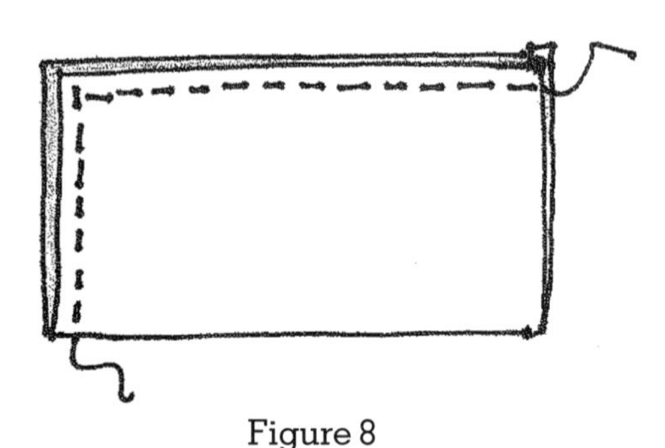

Figure 8

12 Lapping right over left, sew hook and loop tape to the back opening.

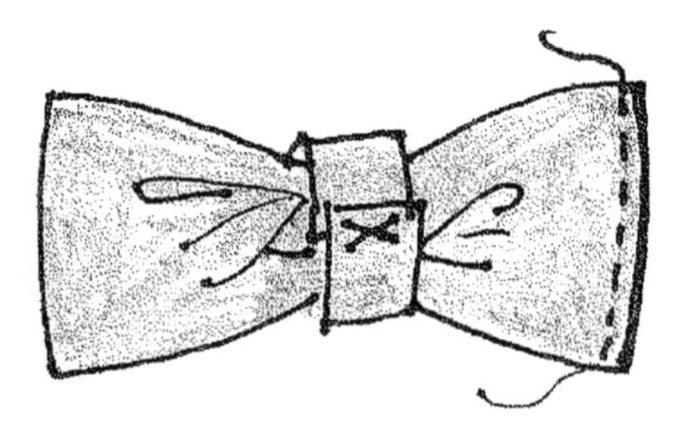

Figure 9

Hat Instructions

1 Cut one hat crown from the black fabric and one from the interfacing. Cut two hat brims from the black fabric.

2 Pin the interfacing to the wrong side of the hat crown and baste the edges together. Treating it as one unit, stitch the side seam of the hat with right sides together. (Figure 10) Trim the ends. Turn right side out.

3 With right sides together, stitch around the outside of the brims. Clip the curves, turn right side out and press.

4 Stitch from the inner brim edges to the lower edges of the crown. Clip the curves, trim the seam allowances to ⅛" (3mm) and press the brim away from the crown. (Figure 11)

5 For the bow, cut a 4" (10cm) square and a 1¼" × 2" (3.2cm × 5.1cm) rectangle from star print fabric. Make the bow in the same manner as in step 11 for the dress. Tack the bow to the front of the hat.

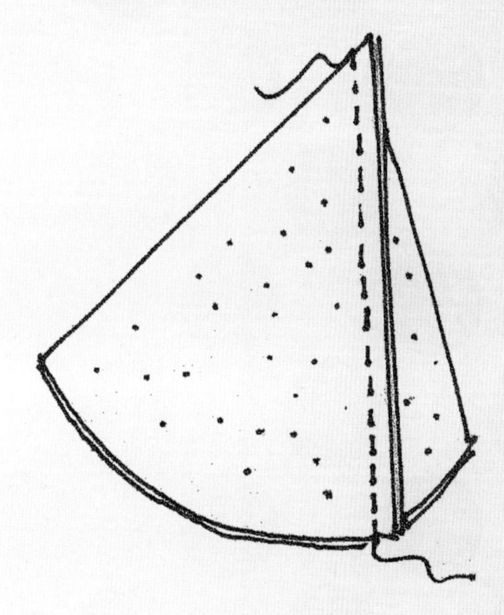

Figure 10

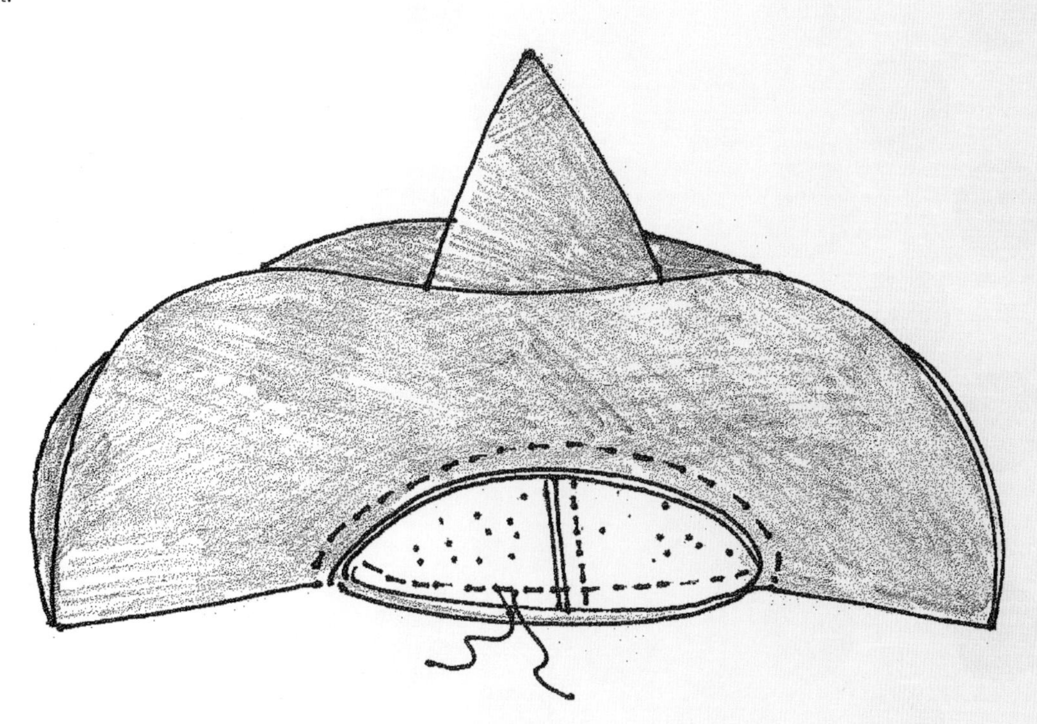

Figure 11

Traditional
Halloween

Pumpkin

Footless Tights, Turtleneck, Pumpkin and Cap

Every doll needs this classic Halloween costume! The green shirt and footless tights are easily made from a stretchy knit fabric. The pumpkin is a lined sleeveless top with elastic in a casing at the lower edge (for a rounder pumpkin, pull the elastic edge up higher on the doll). The face is appliqued with black cotton, but you could glue on a felt face if you prefer. The four-section cap with a felt leaf is literally the crowning touch.

Footless Tights and Turtleneck Supplies

Pumpkin pattern pieces: Turtleneck Front, Turtleneck Back, Turtleneck Sleeve, Footless Tights

⅓ yard (0.3m) green knit fabric (must have two-way stretch)

10" (25.4cm) elastic, ½" (13mm) wide

3" (7.6cm) strip of hook and loop tape, cut lengthwise

Pumpkin and Cap Supplies

Pumpkin pattern pieces: Pumpkin Front, Pumpkin Back, Cap, Leaf, Pumpkin Face

⅓ yard (0.3m) orange cotton fabric

scrap of black fabric

6" × 6" (15.2cm × 15.2cm) paper-backed fusible web

11" (27.9cm) elastic, ½" (13mm) wide

1 snap

15" (38.1cm) of orange single-fold bias tape

scrap of green felt for leaf

3" (7.6cm) long green chenille stem

1½" (3.8cm) long covered wire, 30-gauge

fabric glue

Footless Tights Instructions

Note: if you are using a very stretchy fabric repurposed from human-sized tights, you may want to trim ¼" (6mm) off the bottom of each leg of the doll tights. Zigzag 4" (10.2cm) of ¼" (6mm) elastic across each leg as in step 2. This will give the tights a smoother fit at the ankles.

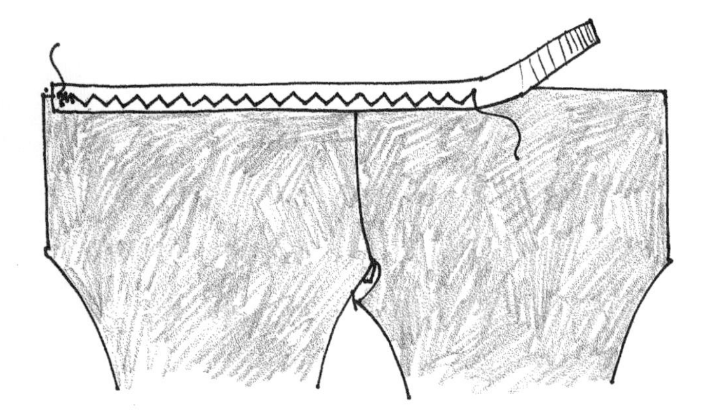

Figure 1

1 Cut two tights from the knit fabric. With right sides together, sew the tights along the center front seam. Press seam allowances open.

2 Place one end of the elastic at the center back seam, overlapping the top edge of the tights. Pull the elastic to the other side as you zigzag stitch it in place. (Figure 1)

3 Press the lower leg edges to the wrong side and topstitch. With right sides together, sew the center back seam.

4 Sew the inner leg seam. (Figure 2)

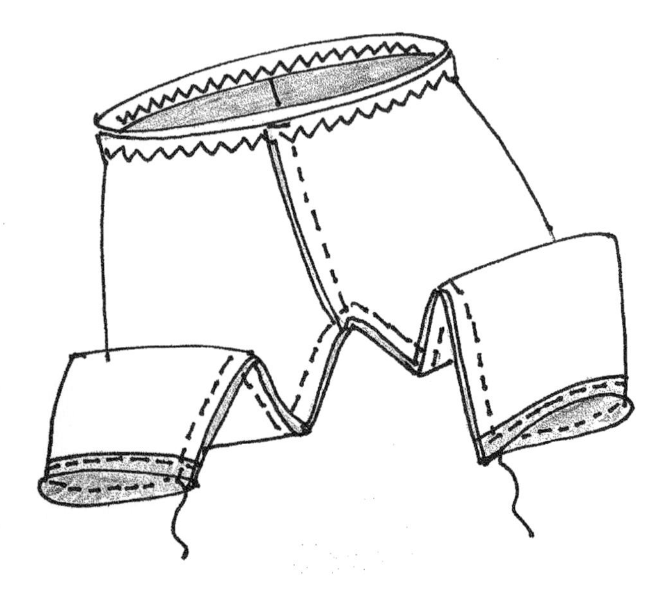

Figure 2

Turtleneck Instructions

1 Cut one front, two backs, two sleeves and one 1½" × 8½" (3.8cm × 22cm) collar from the knit fabric. With right sides together, sew the shoulder seams of the front to the backs. Press the seam allowances open.

2 Press the center back seams ¼" (6mm) to the wrong side and topstitch. With right sides together, fold the collar in half lengthwise and stitch along the short ends. Turn to the right side and press.

3 With right sides together, place the raw edges of the collar along the neckline and stitch. Press seam allowances toward the shirt. (Figure 3)

4 Press the lower sleeve edges ¼" (6mm) to the wrong side and topstitch. With right sides together, sew the sleeve caps to the armholes, easing as necessary. Press the seam allowances to one side.

5 Sew the underarm seam from sleeve edge to the bottom of the shirt. (Figure 4)

6 Press the lower edge of the shirt ¼" (6mm) to the wrong side and topstitch. Lapping right over left, sew the hook and loop tape pieces to the back opening.

Figure 3

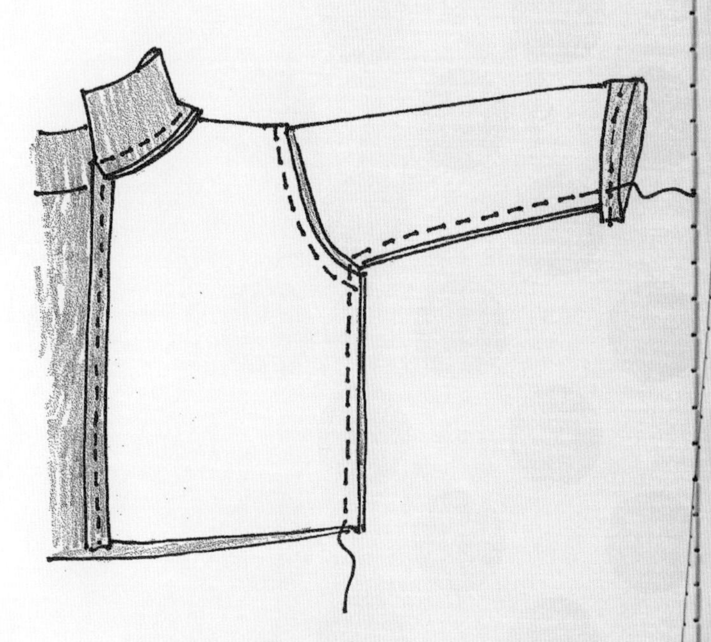

Figure 4

Pumpkin Instructions

1 Cut two fronts and four backs from the orange fabric. Sew the shoulder seams of one front to two backs. Press seam allowances open. Repeat with the remaining pieces for the lining.

2 With right sides together, sew the pumpkin to the lining along the neckline, down the center backs to the dot and around both armholes. (Figure 5) Clip the curves and turn to the right side by pulling the backs to the front through the shoulders. Press.

3 With right sides together, sew the pumpkin backs along the rest of the center back seam. Press seam allowances open. Repeat with the back lining pieces. Turn to the right side and press. (Figure 6)

4 Trace the pumpkin face onto one of the paper sides of the fusible web. Peel the paper off the other side of the web and press onto the black scrap fabric. Cut out each shape and place on the pumpkin front where marked on the pattern piece. Fuse to the pumpkin with an iron, following manufacturer's instructions. Straight stitch around each shape, staying close to the edges.

5 Open out the lining from the pumpkin and, with right sides together, sew the side seams. Press the seam allowances open. (Figure 7)

6 Press the lower edge of both the pumpkin and the lining ¼" (6mm) to the wrong side. Stitch them together close to the pressed edge, leaving a 1" (2.5cm) opening at the center back seam. Stitch ½" (13mm) above the previous stitching, going completely around the lower edge to create a casing. Thread the elastic through the casing and secure the ends. Stitch the opening closed. (Figure 8)

7 Sew the snap at the top of the back opening, lapping right over left.

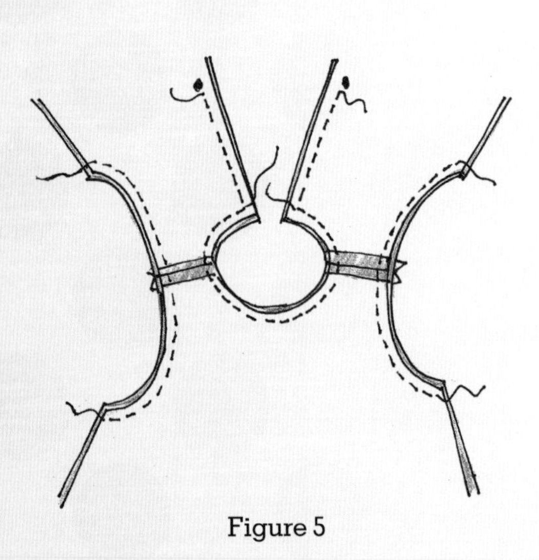

Figure 5

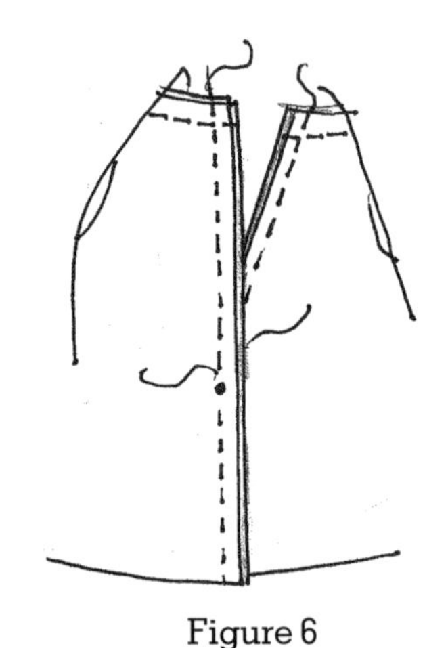

Figure 6

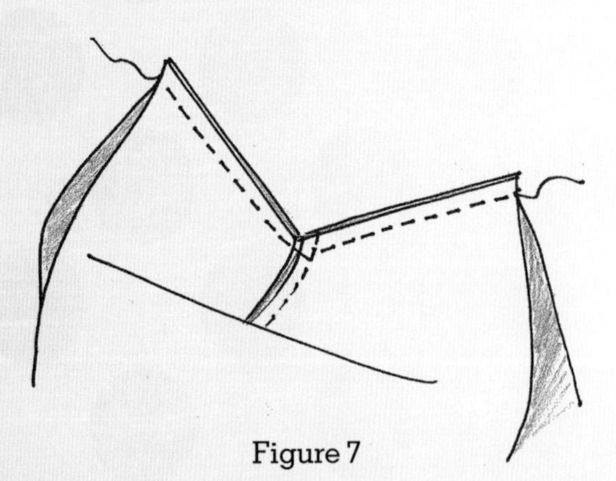

Figure 7

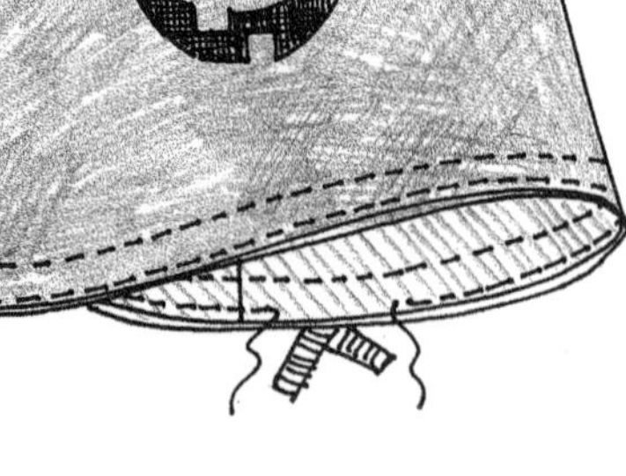

Figure 8

Cap Instructions

1 Cut eight cap sections from the orange fabric.

2 With right sides together, sew two sections from the base to within ¼" (6mm) from the point at the top. Repeat this step three more times.

3 With a pair of cap sections from step 2, sew the seam along the outside edges from the base to the crown, over the point and back down to the base at the other side. Repeat this step with the remaining sections for the lining. Press the seams of the cap and the lining to one side. (Figure 9)

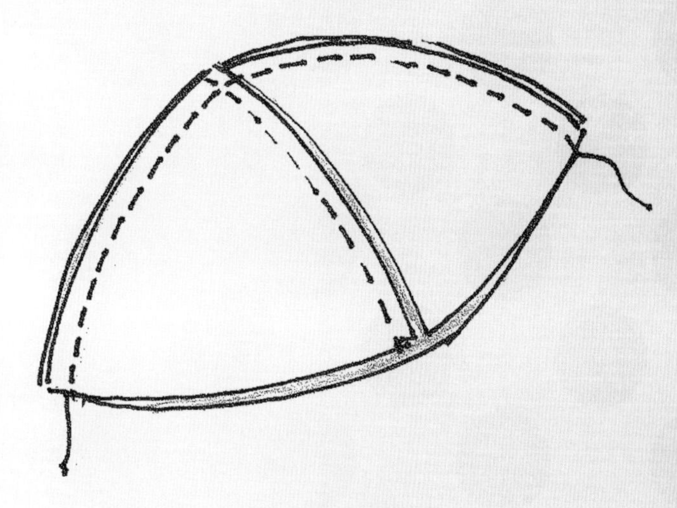

Figure 9

4 Pin the cap and the lining wrong sides together. Open out the bias tape and stitch it to the lower cap edge with right sides together, overlapping the ends. Fold the bias tape to the inside of the cap and stitch in place. (Figure 10)

5 Cut a leaf from the felt. Glue the wire to the underside of the leaf. Curl the chenille stem around a pencil. Clip the stitching at the top of the cap and insert the stem with a small drop of glue to secure. Glue the leaf to base of the stem, curving it slightly.

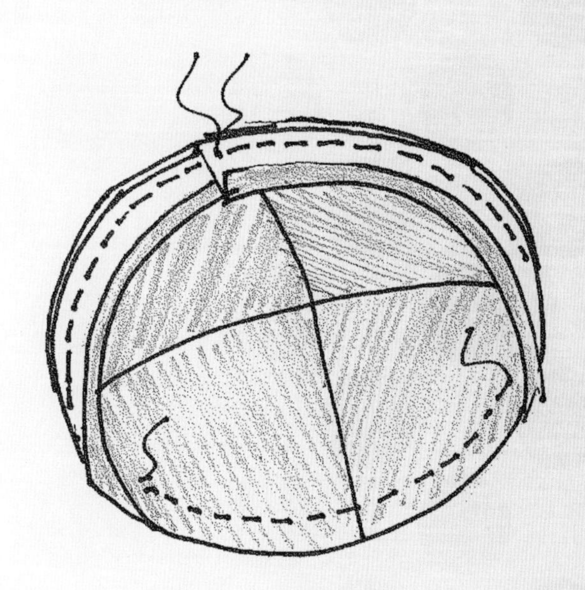

Figure 10

Traditional
Halloween

Kitty Cat

Top, Leggings and Ears

Black cats and Halloween go together like chocolate and peanut butter. Your doll can wear this soft and furry *Kitty Cat* costume for a perfect night of trick-or-treating. The costume is made from knit fabrics and marabou fur trim. This kitty's cute tail and ears are made from different sizes of chenille stems with some special finishing touches.

Top and Leggings Supplies

Kitty Cat pattern pieces: Leggings, Top Front, Top Back, Top Sleeve, Tummy

½ yard (0.5m) black medium-weight knit fabric

scrap white knit fabric (tummy area)

1 marabou feather boa

3" (7.6cm) strip of hook and loop tape, cut lengthwise

11" (27.9cm) elastic, ¼" (6mm) wide

16" (40.6cm) giant chenille stem, about 1½" (3.8cm) wide

Ears Supplies

Kitty Cat pattern pieces: Small Ear, Large Ear

scraps of white and black felt (ears)

two black chenille stems, 6mm wide

fabric glue

Top Instructions

1 Cut one front, two backs and two sleeves. Cut a 1" × 8½" (2.5cm × 21.6cm) strip from the black fabric for the ribbed neckline. Cut one tummy piece from the white fabric.

2 Place the white tummy on the top front as marked on the pattern piece. Zigzag around the edge using white thread. (Figure 1)

3 Serge or zigzag the center back edges. Press the edges ¼" (6mm) to the wrong side and stitch in place. With right sides together, sew the sleeves to the front and the backs.

4 With right sides together, fold the black ribbing in half lengthwise and stitch the ends. Turn the ribbing to the right side and press. Pin the ribbing to the right side of the neckline, stretching as you pin, and serge or zigzag in place. Press the seam allowances toward the body of the garment. (Figure 2)

5 Serge or zigzag along the lower edges of the sleeves. Press the edges to the wrong side and stitch. With right sides together, sew the underarm seam from the sleeve edge to the bottom edge of the top. (Figure 3)

6 Serge or zigzag the bottom edge of the top. Press the edge ¼" (6mm) to the wrong side and stitch.

7 Lapping right over left, sew the hook and loop tape pieces to the back opening.

8 Cut two 4½" (11.4cm) pieces of feather boa for the sleeves, and one 8½" (21.6cm) piece for the neckline. Hand stitch each piece to the sleeve edges and neckline ribbing.

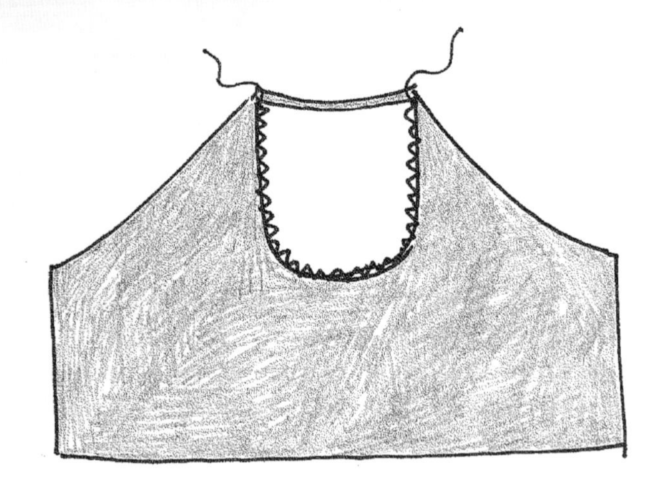

Figure 1

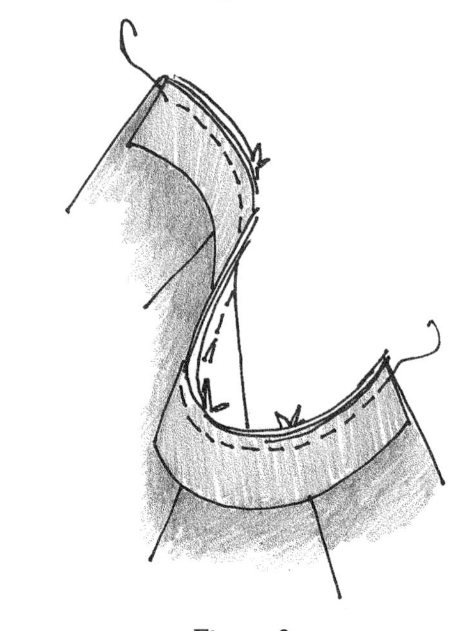

Figure 2

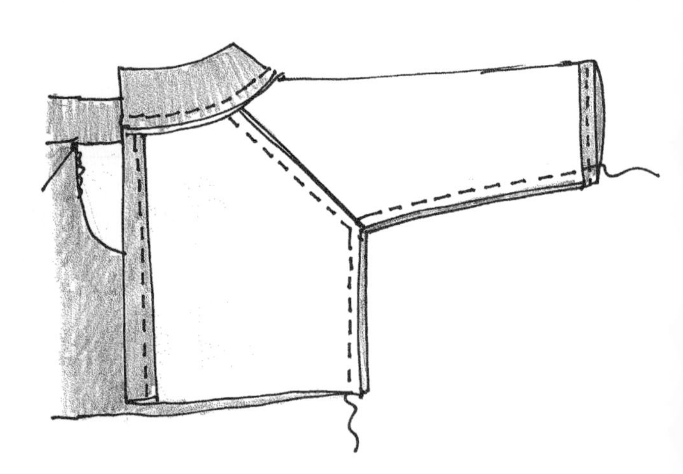

Figure 3

Leggings Instructions

1 Cut two leggings from the black fabric. With right sides together, sew the center front and back seams. Leave a 1" (2.56cm) opening in the center back seam as marked on the pattern piece.

2 Serge or zigzag stitch the lower leg edges. Press the edges ¼" (6mm) to the wrong side and stitch. Sew the inner leg seam.

3 Serge around the waistline. Fold the edge over ½" (3mm) and stitch, leaving a 1" (2.5cm) opening at the back. Thread the piece of 11" (27.9cm) elastic through the casing and stitch the ends together. Stitch the opening closed. (Figure 4)

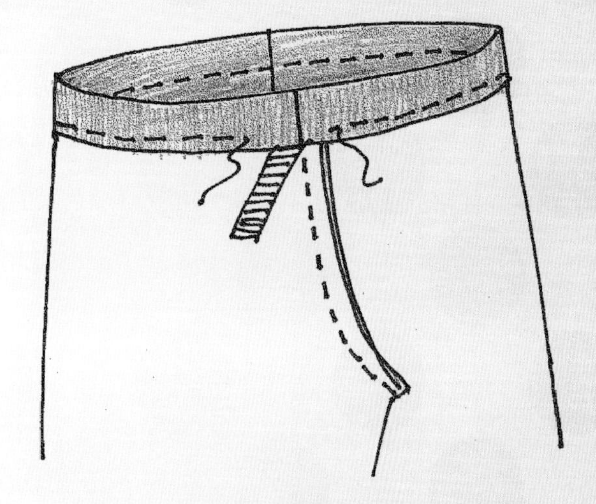

Figure 4

4 Cut two 5" (12.7cm) pieces of feather boa and hand sew them to the bottom of the leggings.

5 For the tail, fold the giant chenille stem in half. Insert the ends into the opening in the back and tack in place. (Figure 5)

Figure 5

Ears Instructions

1 Twist two chenille stems together lightly and cut them at 7½" (19.1cm) long. Curve them to fit the doll's head. Cut two large ears from the black felt and two small ears from the white felt.

2 Glue the white ears to the black ones, making sure the bottom edges are flush. Glue the ears 2" (5.1cm) from each end of the stems. To curve the ears, fold the bottom corners of the ears and glue in place. (Figure 6)

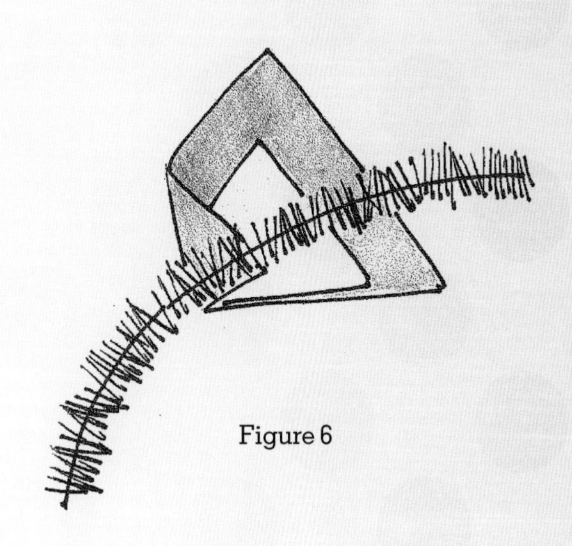

Figure 6

Variation: Leopard

Top, Leggings and Ears

This leopard print knit fabric is just the right scale to create a *Leopard* costume. The pattern pieces are the same as those used in the *Kitty Cat* costume. The marabou trim has been eliminated, and the black knit is used for the "tummy" and the ribbing at the neck. Keep the fat chenille stem for a tail.

Top and Leggings Supplies

Kitty Cat pattern pieces: Leggings, Top Front, Top Back, Top Sleeve, Tummy

½ yard (0.5m) medium-weight knit fabric

scrap of black knit fabric (tummy area and neck)

11" (27.9cm) elastic, ¼" (6mm) wide

3" (7.6cm) strip of hook and loop tape, cut lengthwise

16" (41cm) giant chenille stem, about 1½" (3.8cm) wide

Ears Supplies

Kitty Cat pattern pieces: Small Ear, Large Ear

scraps of pink and black felt for ears

two black chenille stems, 6mm wide

fabric glue

Top Instructions

Follow the instructions for the *Kitty Cat* costume, eliminating step 8. Cut the tummy section and the ribbed neckline strip from black knit fabric.

Leggings Instructions

Follow the instructions for the *Kitty Cat* Leggings, eliminating step 4.

Ears Instructions

Follow the instructions for the *Kitty Cat* ears. Use the pink felt for the inner ear.

Variations: Dog and Mouse

The pattern pieces for the *Kitty Cat* are adaptable for other animals. Make a dog costume from a Dalmatian print or other knit fabrics. For a mouse, make the costume from white or gray knits with a pink tummy. The tails for both costumes can be a small chenille stem instead of a large one. Try these patterns to make ears for a dog and a mouse.

Dog Ears Supplies:

- *Dog* pattern pieces: Ear
- scraps of brown or black felt for ears
- two brown or black chenille stems, 6mm wide

Dog Ears Instructions

1 Coil two chenille stems together lightly and cut them at 7½" (19.1cm) long. Curve them to fit the doll's head. Cut two ears from the felt.

2 Make a small pleat in the straight end of the ears so that the edge measures ½" (13mm) wide. Place the ears 1½" (3.8cm) from the ends of the headband, and hand stitch them to the back side of the headband. They will fold over the headband when placed on the doll.

Mouse Ears Supplies:

- *Mouse* pattern pieces: Small Ear, Large Ear
- scraps of white and pink felt for ears
- two white chenille stems, 6mm wide
- fabric glue

Mouse Ears Instructions

1 Coil two chenille stems together lightly and cut them 7½" (19.1cm) long. Curve them to fit the doll's head. Cut two large ears from the white felt and two small ears from the pink felt.

2 Glue the pink ears to the white ones, making sure the bottom edges are flush. Make a tiny pleat in the bottom of the ears. Glue the ears 2" (5.1cm) from the end of each stem.

Traditional Halloween

Clown

Jacket, Pants, Hat and Shoes

Performing under the big top is a lot of fun in this classic *Clown* costume. Use stripes and polka-dot fabrics with lots of ball fringe and rickrack. Her big shoes are simple to make from felt and pompoms. Find a few balls for juggling, and let the show begin.

Jacket, Pants and Hat Supplies

- *Clown* pattern pieces: Jacket Front, Jacket Back, Jacket Sleeve, Pants, Hat
- ⅓ yard (0.3m) striped cotton fabric
- ⅓ yard (0.3m) polka-dot cotton fabric
- ½ yard (0.5m) elastic, ⅛" (3mm) wide
- 6 small snaps
- ⅔ yard (0.6m) yellow pompom trim
- ⅔ yard (0.6m) pink pompom trim
- ¼ yard (0.2m) white fabric (collar)
- 1 package of white single-fold bias tape
- 11" (27.9cm) elastic, ⅜" (10mm) wide
- 1 package of medium rickrack
- ⅓ yard (0.3m) elastic, ¼" (6mm) wide
- 1 yellow pompom, size 1" (2.5cm)

Shoes Supplies

- *Clown* pattern pieces: Shoe Upper, Shoe Sole
- 1 square of craft felt
- 6 small pompoms for the shoes
- fabric glue

Jacket Instructions

1 Cut one front, one back and one sleeve from the striped fabric. Turn the pattern pieces over and cut one front, one back and one sleeve from the polka-dot fabric.

2 With right sides together, sew the back pieces together along the center back seam. (Figure 1)

3 With right sides together, sew the striped front to the striped back and the polka-dot front to the polka-dot back at the shoulders. Press seam allowances open.

4 Serge or zigzag the neckline edge, press under ¼" (6mm) to the wrong side and stitch.

5 Serge or zigzag the center front edges, press under ½" (13mm) to the wrong side, and stitch. (Figure 2)

6 Place the rickrack on the right side along the lower edge of each sleeve so that the edge of the rickrack aligns with the raw edge. Stitch in the center of the rickrack. Press up the hem so one half of the rick rack shows on the edge. Topstitch in place.

7 Cut a 3½" (8.9cm) piece of the ⅛" (3mm) elastic for each sleeve. Starting on one side of each sleeve and ½" (13mm) from the hemmed edge, zigzag over the elastic being careful not to stitch into the elastic as you stretch the elastic to the other side of the sleeve. Secure the elastic at each end. (Figure 3)

8 Gather the sleeve caps between the dots marked on the pattern pieces. Sew the sleeve caps to the armholes. Sew the underarm seam from the sleeve edges to the bottom of the jacket. (Figure 4)

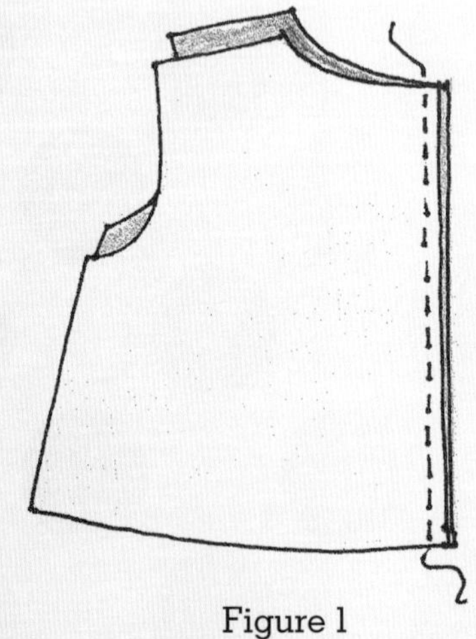

Figure 1

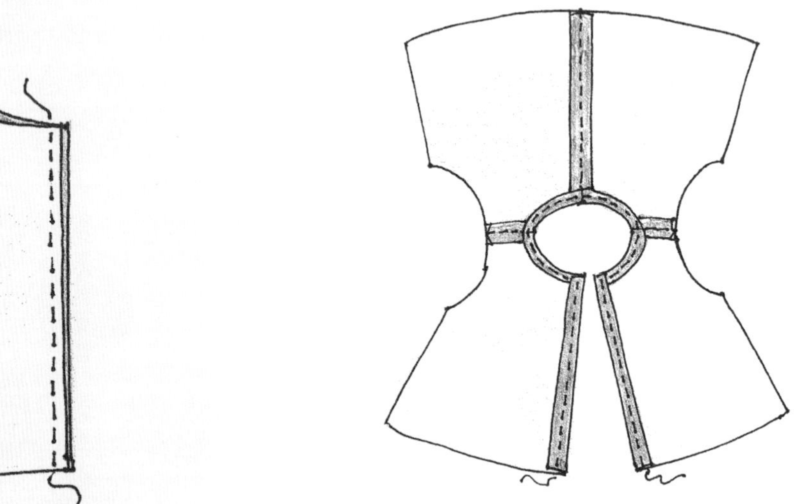

Figure 2

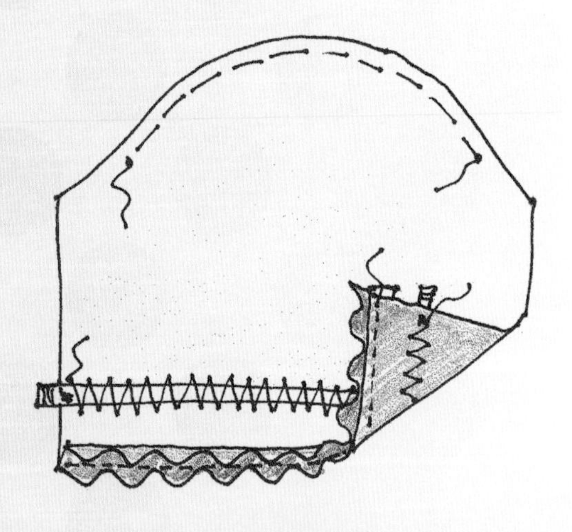

Figure 3

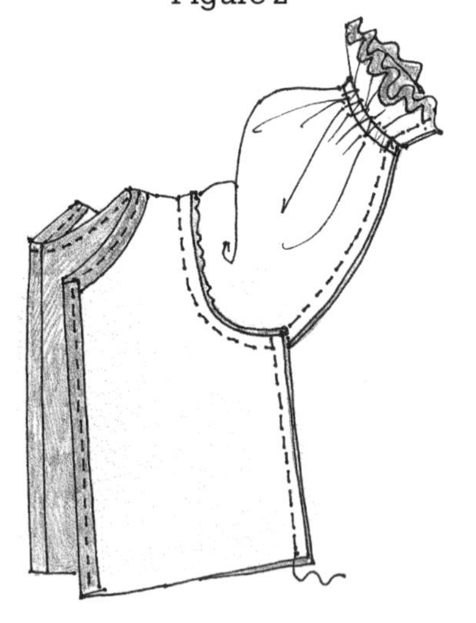

Figure 4

9 Serge or zigzag the lower edge of the jacket. Press the edge ½" (13mm) to the wrong side and stitch.

10 Sew five of the snaps to the front opening as marked on the pattern piece, lapping right over left. Cut two yellow pompoms and one pink pompom from the trim and glue them over the bottom three snaps on the right half of the jacket.

11 For the collar, cut two 1¾" × 21" (4.4cm × 53.3cm) strips and a 1" × 8½" (2.5cm × 21.6cm) bias strip from the white fabric. Place the two pompom trims together so that the colors alternate. Pin the trim to one long edge, matching the trim heading with the raw edge. With right sides together, pin the two strips together and stitch. (Figure 5) Turn to the right side.

12 Stitch a row of rickrack to the right side of the collar ¼" (6mm) above the pompom trim. (Figure 6)

13 Press the ends of the collar ¼" (6mm) to the wrong side and stitch.

14 Gather the opposite edge of the collar to fit the bias tape strip.

15 Press one long edge of the bias strip ¼" (6mm) to the wrong side. With right sides together, pin and stitch the unpressed edge of the bias to the collar so that the short ends of the binding extend ¼" (6mm) beyond the collar. Fold the binding to the right side and topstitch, enclosing the short ends. (Figure 7)

16 Sew a snap to each end of the collar, lapping right over left.

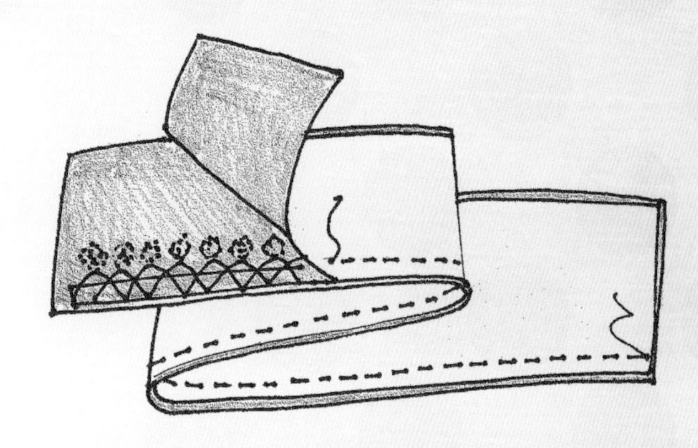

Figure 5

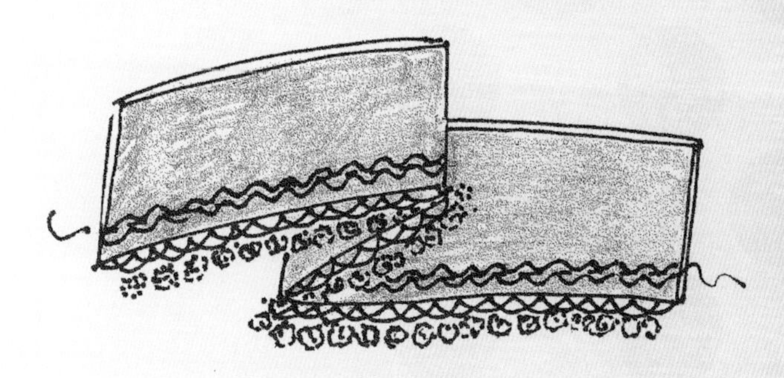

Figure 6

Figure 7

Pants Instructions

1 Cut two pants pieces from the striped fabric and two pants pieces from the polka-dot fabric.

2 With right sides together, sew the striped pants pieces along the side seam. (Figure 8) Repeat for the polka-dot side.

3 Sew the center front and center back seams with right sides together.

4 Stitch the rickrack on the right side along the bottom edge of each pant leg. Press the rickrack to the wrong side and topstitch.

5 Cut 4½" (11.4cm) of the ⅛" (3mm) elastic for each pant leg. Starting at one side of the pant leg and ½" (13mm) from the hemmed edge, zigzag over the elastic, stretching the elastic to the other side of the pant leg. Do not catch the elastic in your stitching except to secure both ends. (Figure 9)

6 Press the top of the pants ¼" (6mm) to the wrong side. Press ½" (13mm) again to the wrong side and stitch, leaving a 1" (2.5cm) opening at the back. Thread the ⅜" (10mm) elastic in the casing and secure the ends. Stitch the opening closed.

7 Sew the inner leg seam. (Figure 10)

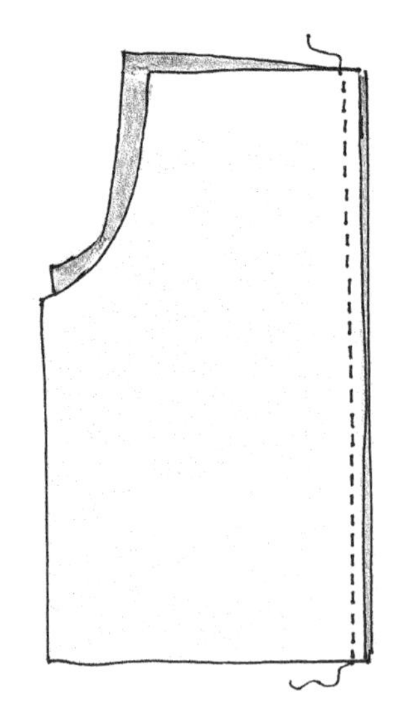

Figure 8

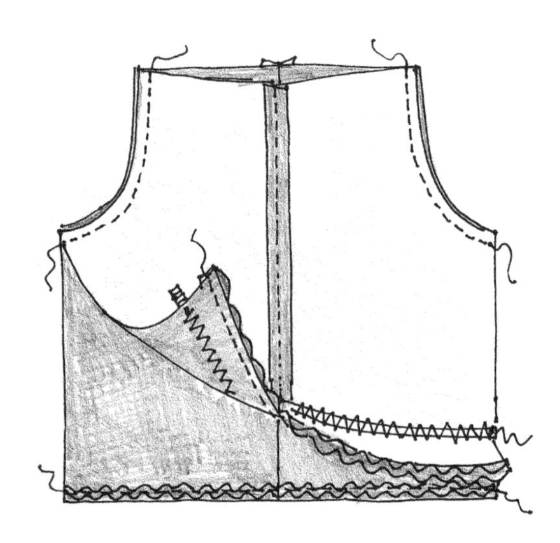

Figure 9

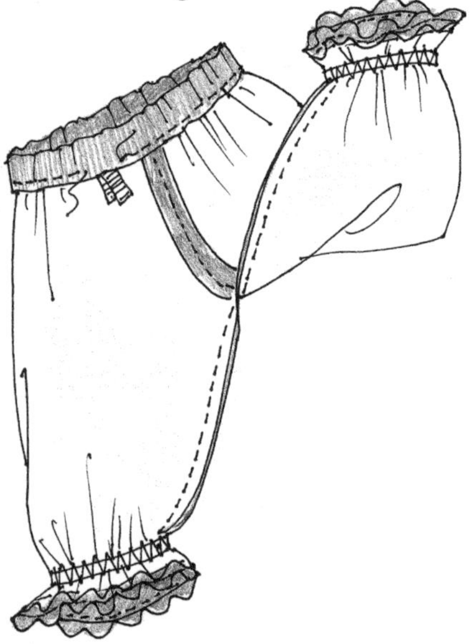

Figure 10

Hat Instructions

1 Cut one hat from the striped fabric and one from the polka-dot fabric. With right sides together, sew the hat pieces along the side edges. (Figure 11)

2 Cut a piece of bias tape to fit the lower edge of the hat, plus an additional ½" (13mm). Open out one side of the bias tape, and with right sides together, stitch it to the lower edge of the hat, overlapping the ends. Fold the tape to the wrong side of the hat and stitch, leaving a 1" (2.5cm) opening. Insert the ¼" (6mm) elastic in the casing and secure the ends. Stitch the opening closed.

3 Stitch the large pompom to the end of the hat. (Figure 12)

Shoes Instructions

1 Cut two shoe uppers and two soles from the felt.

2 With right sides together, sew the center back seam of each upper. (Figure 13) Press the seam allowances open. Turn to the right side.

3 Place the wrong side of the upper to the wrong side of the sole. Stitch along the outer edge. Topstitch along the stitching lines as marked on the pattern piece. Repeat with the second shoe. (Figure 14)

4 Glue three evenly placed pompoms down the center of each shoe.

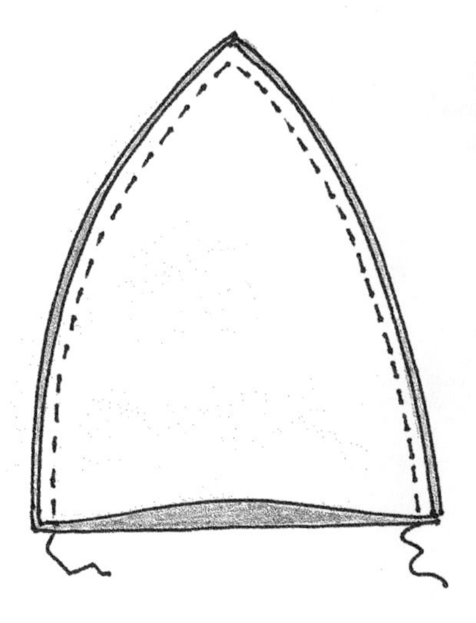

Figure 11

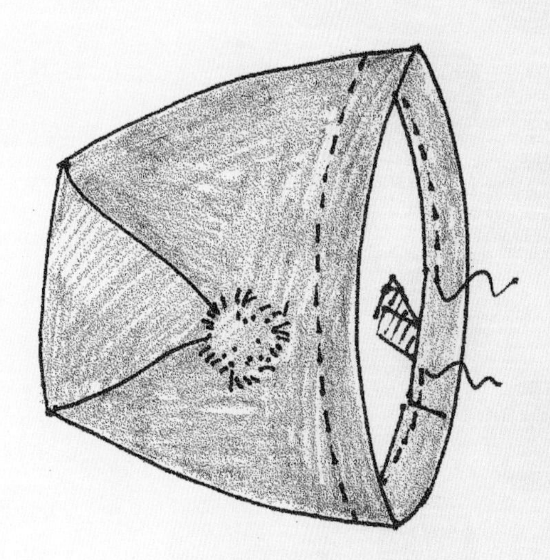

Figure 12

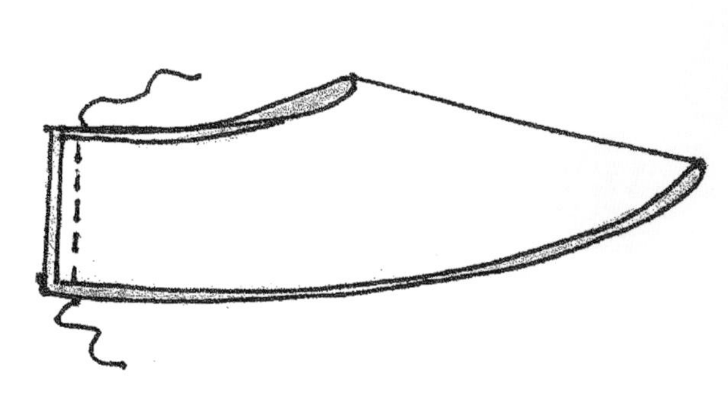

Figure 13

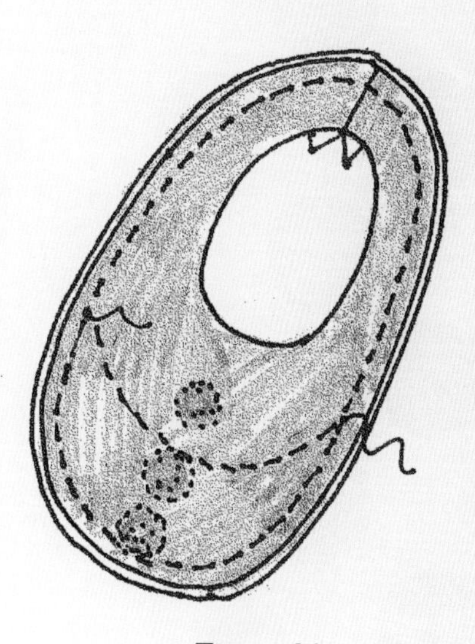

Figure 14

Playtime

Pirate

Shirt, Pants, Vest, Belt, Head Scarf and Eye Patch

Your doll can rule the high seas as a pirate! She wears a white shirt with an old-fashioned placket in the front and a long pointed collar. The simple pull-on pants tuck into her tall black boots. The vest has large pockets and closes at the front with a belt. Don't forget the eye patch to finish the costume.

Shirt and Vest Supplies

Pirate pattern pieces: Shirt Front, Shirt Back, Shirt Sleeve, Shirt Collar, Vest Front, Vest Back

¼ yard (0.2m) white cotton fabric (shirt)

1 package of white single-fold bias tape

6" (15.2cm) elastic, ⅛" (3mm) wide

3" (7.6cm) strip of hook and loop tape

¼ yard (0.2m) red or burgundy cotton fabric (vest)

Pants Supplies

Pirate pattern pieces: Pants

⅓ yard (0.3m) striped cotton fabric (pants)

11" (27.9cm) elastic, ¼" (6mm) wide

Belt, Head Scarf and Eye Patch Supplies

Pirate pattern pieces: Scarf, Eye Patch

16" (40.6cm) ribbon, ⅝" (16mm) wide (belt)

seam sealant

⅞" (22mm) belt buckle

¼ yard (0.2m) black cotton fabric (cap)

scrap of felt

10" (25.4cm) black elastic strip, ¼" (6mm) wide

Shirt Instructions

1 Cut one front, two backs, four collars and two sleeves from the white fabric. Cut a 3" (7.6cm) piece of white bias tape for the slit in the front.

2 Cut a slit along the center front of the shirt 1¼" (3.2cm) from the neckline. Pull the sides apart so that the slit is almost straight. Open out one side of the bias tape and place it along the slit with right sides together. Stitch with a ¼" (6mm) seam allowance at the beginning and gradually taper to 2–3 threads at the end of the slit. Pivot your needle and begin stitching the other side of the slit, starting with a narrow seam allowance and ending with a ¼" (6mm) seam allowance. (Figure 1) Press the tape over to the wrong side and topstitch.

3 With right sides together, sew the shoulder seams. Press them open. Press the center back edges ¼" (6mm) to the wrong side. Press them under another ¼" (6mm) and stitch in place. (Figure 2)

4 Place two collar sections right sides together and stitch around all sides except the straight edge. Trim the points, turn to the right side and press. Repeat with the remaining collar sections. (Figure 3) Pin the collars to the neckline with the longest point in line with the front slit. Baste the collars in place.

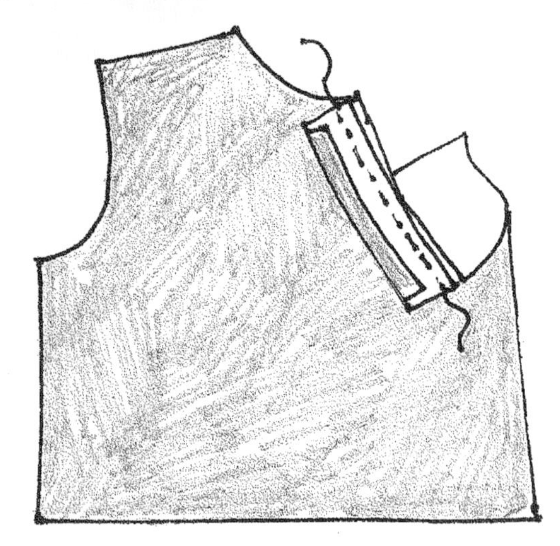

Figure 1

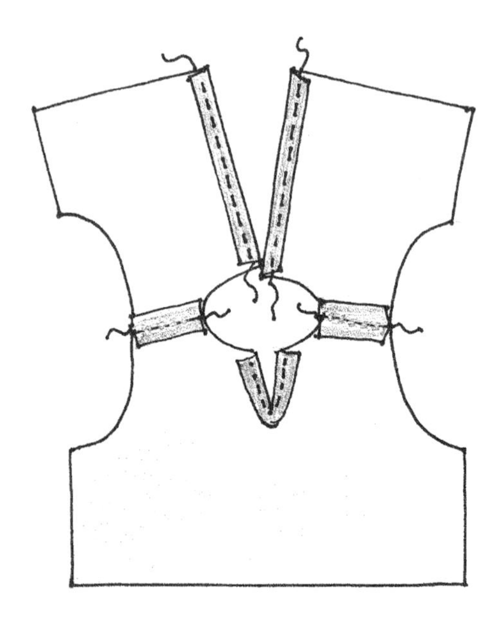

Figure 2

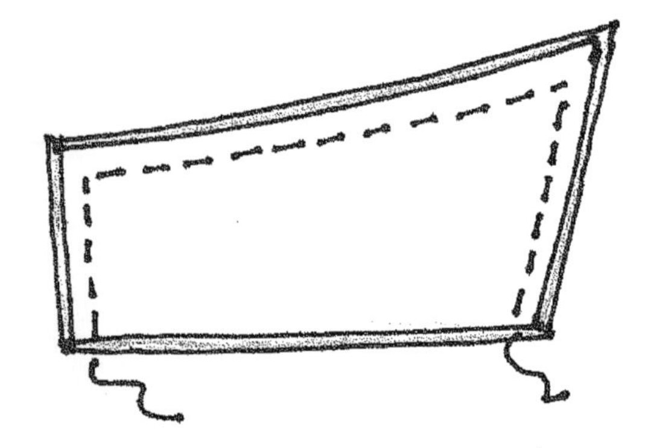

Figure 3

5 Cut two pieces of bias tape to fit around the neckline edges with ¼" (6mm) extra on each end. Open out one side of the tape and stitch it to one of the neckline edges, right sides together. Fold the tape to the wrong side and stitch, tucking in the ends. Repeat with the other neckline edge. (Figure 4)

6 Press the lower edge of the sleeves ¼" (6mm) to the wrong side. Press under another ¼" (6mm) and stitch in place. Cut the ⅛" (3mm) elastic into two pieces. Starting at one side of the sleeve and ½" (13mm) up from the lower edge, stitch over the elastic with a wide zigzag stitch, only catching the ends of the elastic at each side of the sleeve. Repeat with the other sleeve. (Figure 5)

7 Gather the top edges of each sleeve cap between the marks to fit the armhole. With right sides together, sew the sleeve to the armhole. Press.

8 Starting from the sleeve edge, sew the underarm seams. (Figure 6)

9 Press the lower edge of the shirt ¼" (6mm) to the wrong side. Press under another ¼" (6mm) and stitch in place. Lapping right over left, sew the hook and loop tape to the back opening.

Figure 4

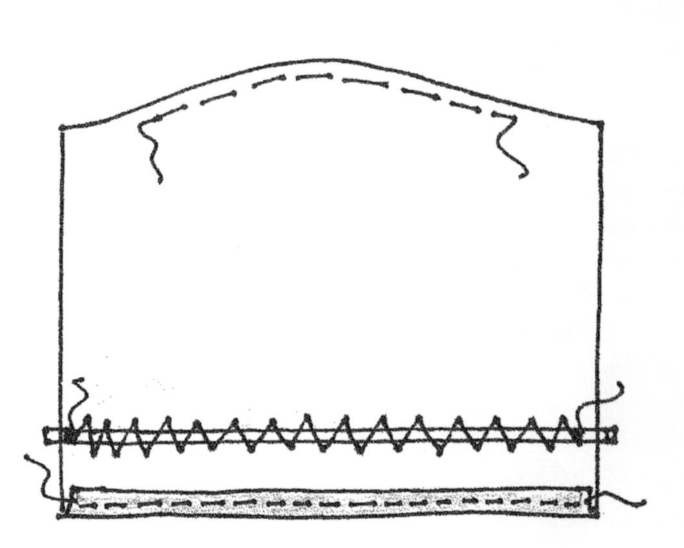

Figure 5

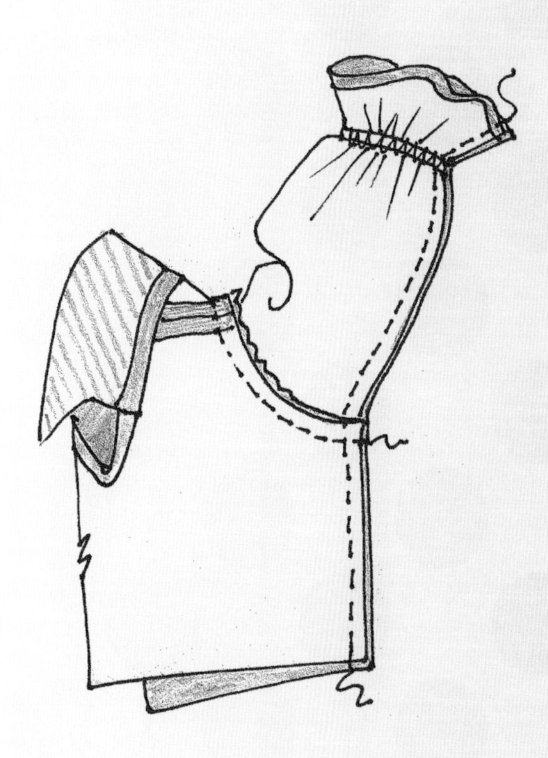

Figure 6

Pants Instructions

1 Cut four pants pieces from the striped fabric.

2 With the right sides of two pants pieces together, sew the center front seam. Sew a remaining pants piece to each side of the front along a side seam. Leave the center back seam open. (Figure 7)

3 Serge or zigzag the top edge of the pants. Press this edge ½" (13mm) to the wrong side and stitch ⅜" (10mm) from the pressed edge to create a casing. Thread the ¼" (6mm) elastic through the casing and secure it at each end. (Figure 8) Sew the center back seam.

4 Serge or zigzag the pant leg edges. Press the pant hem ¼" (6mm) to the wrong side and stitch in place. Sew the inner leg seam. (Figure 9)

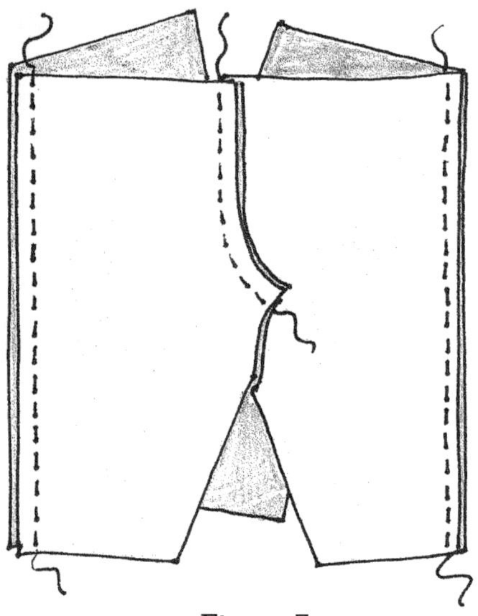

Figure 7

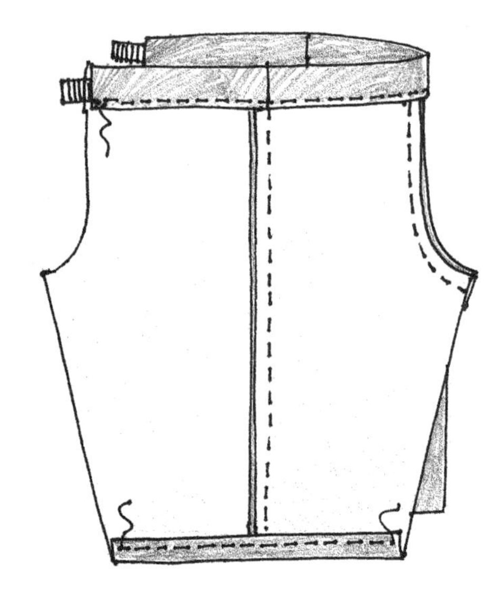

Figure 8

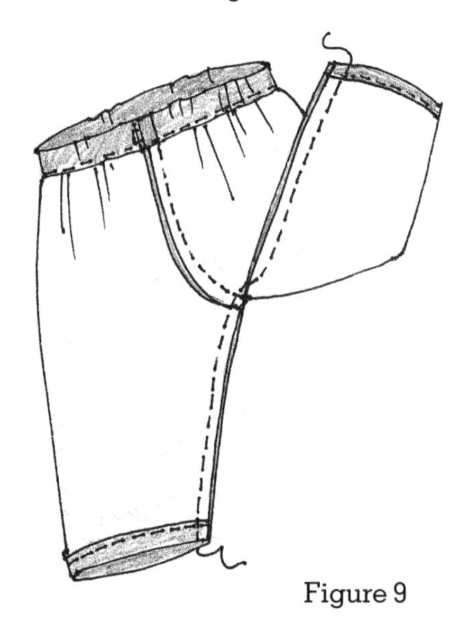

Figure 9

Vest Instructions

1 Cut four fronts, two backs and two 2½" × 7½" (6cm × 19cm) pockets from the red or burgundy fabric.

2 With right sides together, sew two fronts to one back at the shoulders. Press seam allowances open. Repeat with the remaining pieces for the lining. (Figure 10)

3 Place the lining to the vest with right sides together and stitch across the bottom front edge, up one side of the center front, around the neckline, down the other center front and across the other bottom front. Stitch around each armhole and across the lower back edge. (Figure 11) Clip the curves, turn to the right side and press.

4 With right sides together, fold each pocket in half so they measure 2½" × 3¾" (6cm × 10cm). Stitch around all sides of each pocket, leaving a small opening along one side. (Figure 12) Turn to the right side and press. Also press under the edges of the opening. Create a flap by pressing down one narrow edge 1" (3cm).

Figure 10

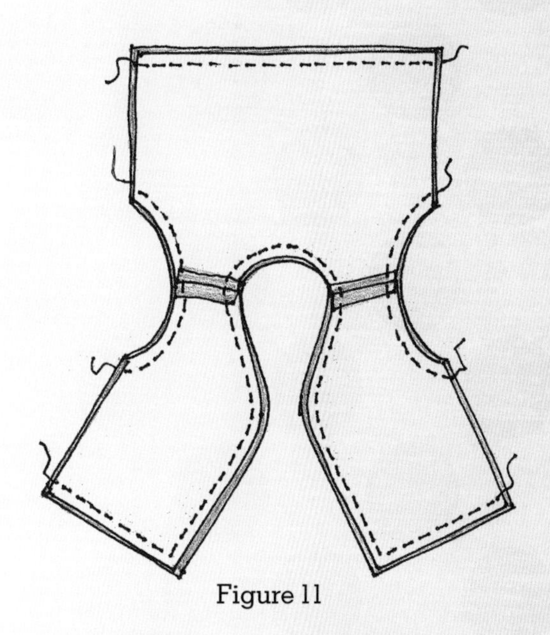

Figure 11

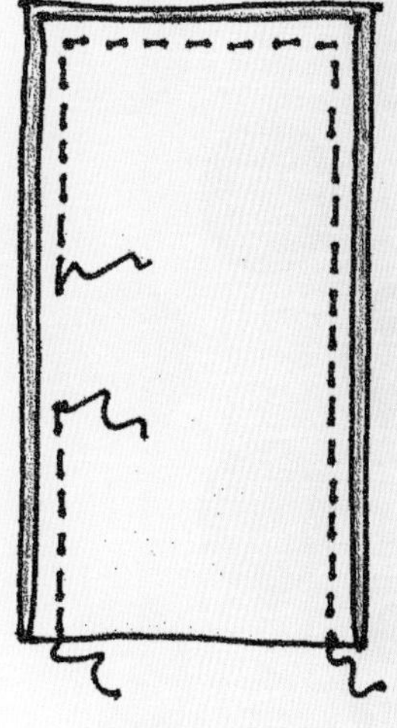

Figure 12

5 Pin the pockets to the vest ¼" (6mm) from the bottom edge and 1¼" (3.2cm) from the center front edge. Stitch the pockets to the vest, sewing around the sides and bottom. (Figure 13)

6 With right sides together, sew the vest side seams. (Figure 14)

Belt Instructions

1 Seal the ends of the black ribbon with seam sealant. Make a hole in the ribbon approximately ½" (13mm) from one end. Fold the end over the center of the buckle, placing the stem in the hole. Glue the end to the underside of the belt.

2 Make a hole in the center of the ribbon 2½" (6.4cm) from the other end. (Figure 15)

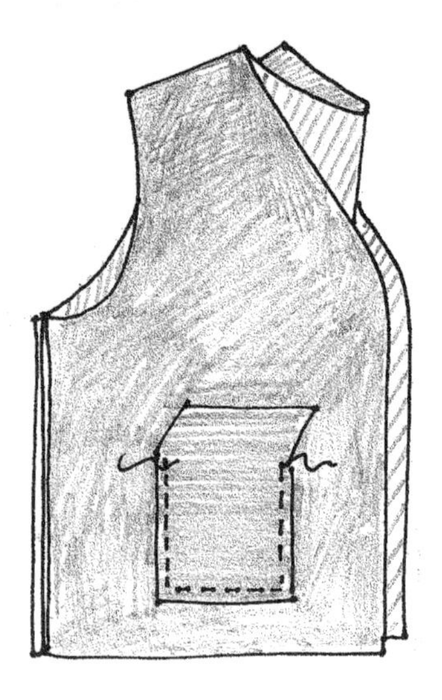

Figure 13

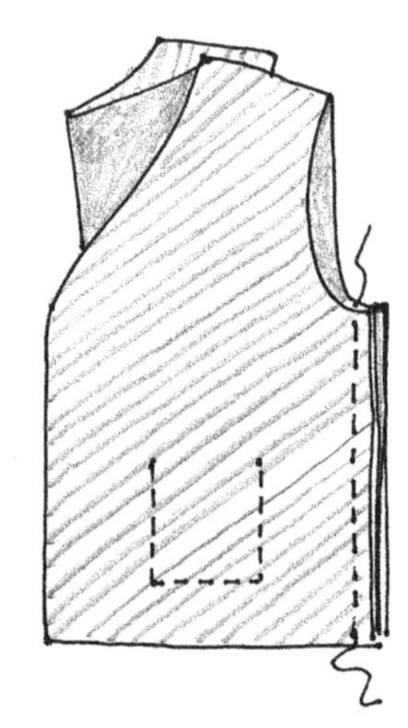

Figure 14

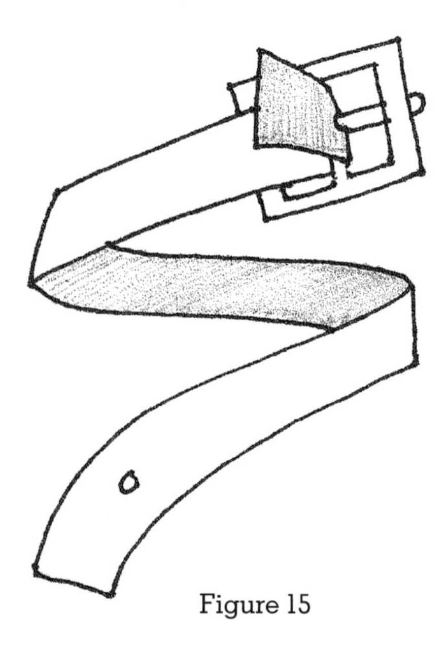

Figure 15

Head Scarf Instructions

1 Cut one scarf from the black fabric. Press the long bottom edge, the long edges of the ties and the ends ¼" (6mm) to the wrong side. Stitch in place (Figure 16).

2 With right sides together, sew each dart in the head scarf. Then fold the cap in half with right sides together and matching the darts and raw edges.

3 Stitch along the curved edge creating a cap. (The stitching does not extend all the way to the lower edge.) (Figure 17)

4 Place the cap on the doll's head and tie the ends in a knot.

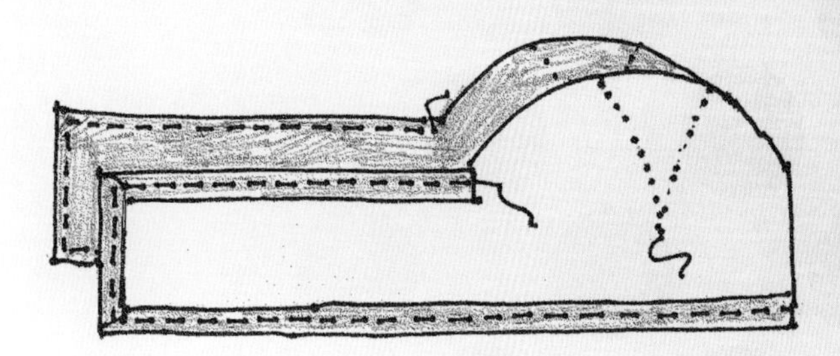

Figure 16

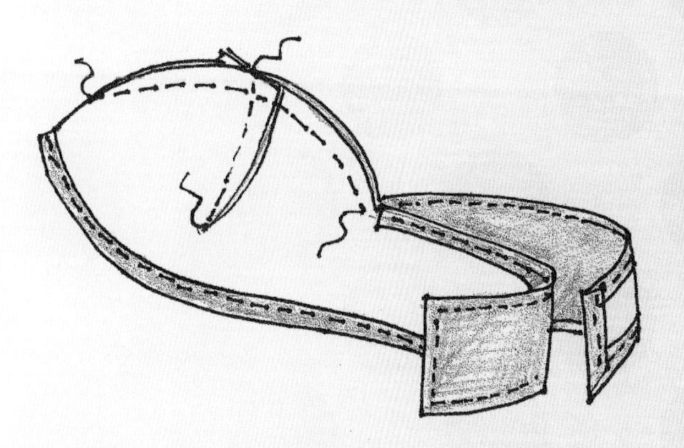

Figure 17

Eye Patch Instructions

1 Cut two eye patches from the scrap of felt.

2 Stitch the ends of the black elastic to the sides of the felt as marked on the pattern piece. Place the second patch on top, enclosing the ends of the elastic between the two patches. Topstitch around the edge. (Figure 18)

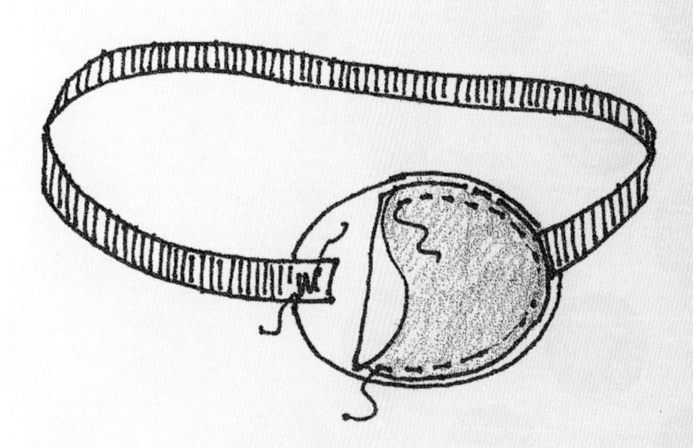

Figure 18

Playtime

Mermaid

Fishtail, Top and Hair Clip

Your doll will look as though she is ready to jump into the ocean in this glamorous mermaid costume. The fishtail, made from a shiny knit fabric, is constructed just like a skirt. It has an elastic waist, tail extension on one side, and a split in the seam for your doll's legs. You can pad the tail with polyester stuffing to keep it stiff, if you like. The top has an iridescent fabric layer on top of satin with a peplum attached at the waistline. Add a barrette with ribbons and a real shell for the perfect accessory.

Fishtail Supplies

Mermaid pattern pieces: Fishtail

⅓ yard (0.3m) aqua or green sequin knit fabric

⅓ yard (0.3m) aqua or green medium-weight cotton fabric (lining)

11" (27.9cm) elastic, ¼" (6mm) wide

Top Supplies

Mermaid pattern pieces: Top, Peplum

¼ yard (0.2m) satin fabric

¼ yard (0.2m) matching sheer iridescent fabric

20" (50.8cm) pompom trim, ½" (13mm) wide

1 yard (0.9m) decorative trim, ⅜" (10mm) wide

1" (2.5cm) strip of hook and loop tape, cut in half

Hair Clip Supplies

1 yard (0.9m) satin ribbon, ¼" (6mm) wide

1 barrette, 1½" (3.8cm) long

1 shell

fabric glue

hand sewing needle

Fishtail Instructions

1 Cut two fishtails from both the sequin fabric and the cotton lining fabric.

2 With right sides together, sew the side seams and bottom edge of the fishtail, leaving an opening at the bottom unsewn, as marked on the pattern piece. Turn to the right side and press. Repeat with the lining, but don't turn to the right side. (Figure 1)

3 With wrong sides together, insert the lining inside the fishtail. Zigzag or serge the top edges together.

4 Working with the sequin fabric and lining together, fold the edges of the turning hole ¼" (6mm) to the wrong side and machine stitch together. (Figure 2)

5 Fold the top of the fishtail ½" (13mm) to the lining side and stitch, leaving a 1" (2.5cm) opening for the elastic. Thread the elastic through the casing and secure the edges. Sew the opening closed. (Figure 3)

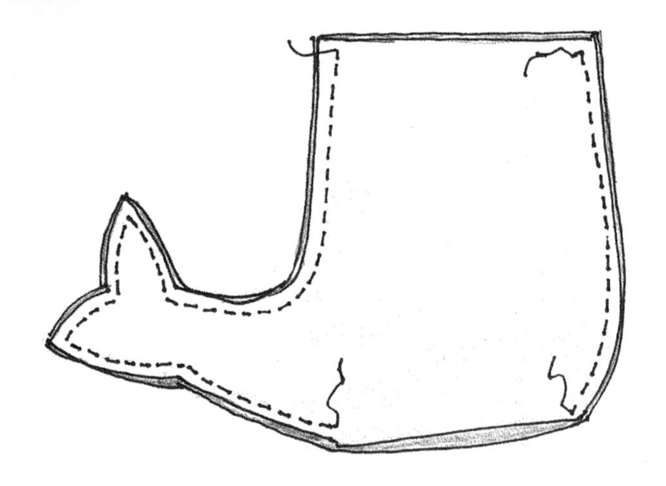

Figure 1

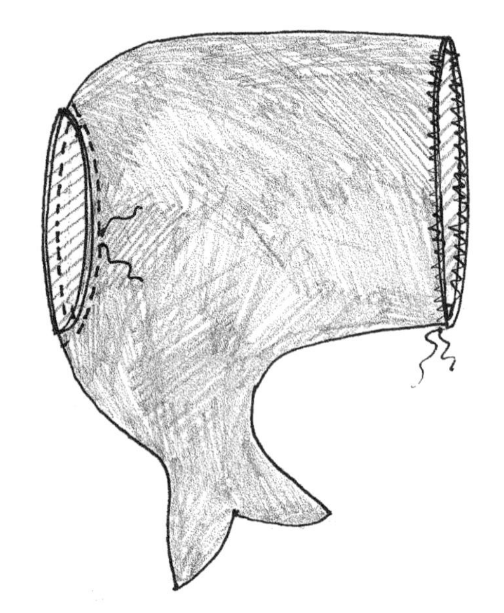

Figure 2

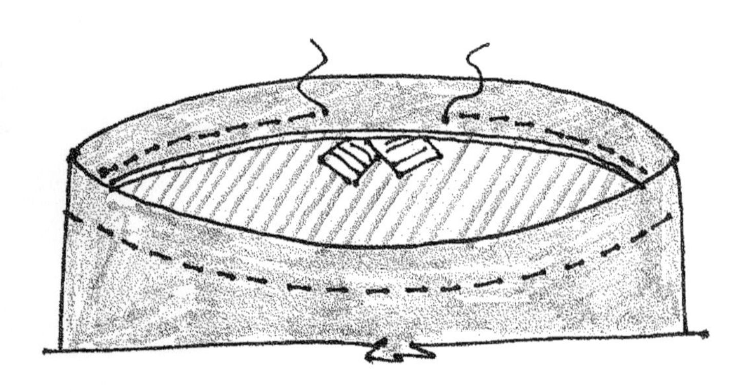

Figure 3

Top Instructions

1 Cut two tops and two peplums from the satin. Cut one top and two peplums from the iridescent fabric.

2 Place the iridescent top on the right side of a satin top. Baste around the edges if desired. With right sides together, sew the remaining satin top to the iridescent/satin top around both ends and the curved top edge. Turn to the right side and press. (Figure 4)

3 Place the iridescent peplums on the right side of each satin peplum. Serge or zigzag along the lower curved edges. (Figure 5) Press the edges ¼" (6mm) to the wrong side. Place the heading of the pompom trim along the pressed edge and stitch in place. (Figure 6)

Figure 4

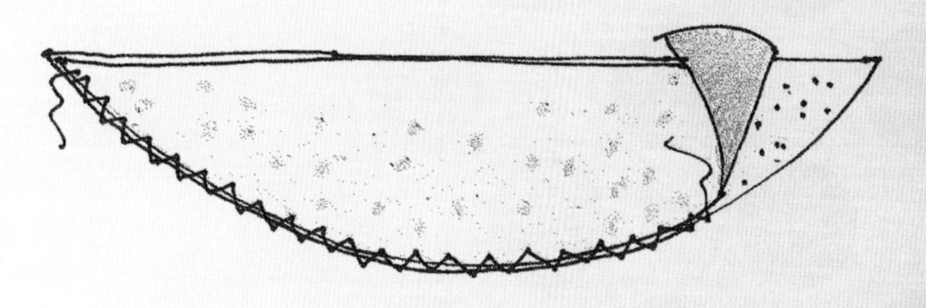

Figure 5

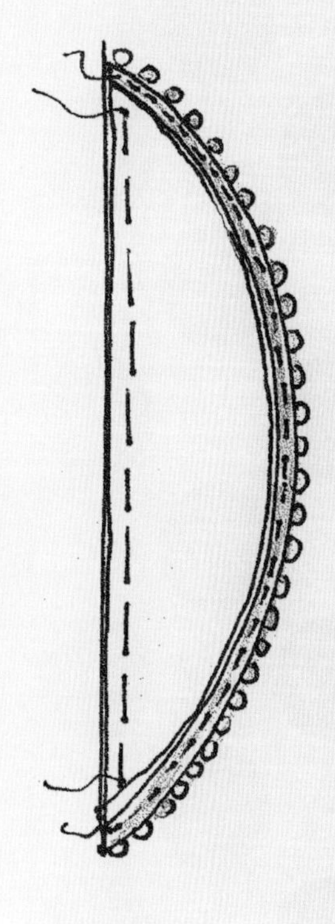

Figure 6

4 Gather the top edge of the peplums and stitch to the lower edge of the top. They should meet at the center of the top and the back edges. Press seam allowances away from the peplum. (Figure 7)

5 Stitch decorative trim to the upper edge of the top, folding the ends underneath the back edges. Stitch trim over the top/peplum seam in the same manner. (Figure 8)

6 Lapping right over left, sew hook and loop tape to the back opening.

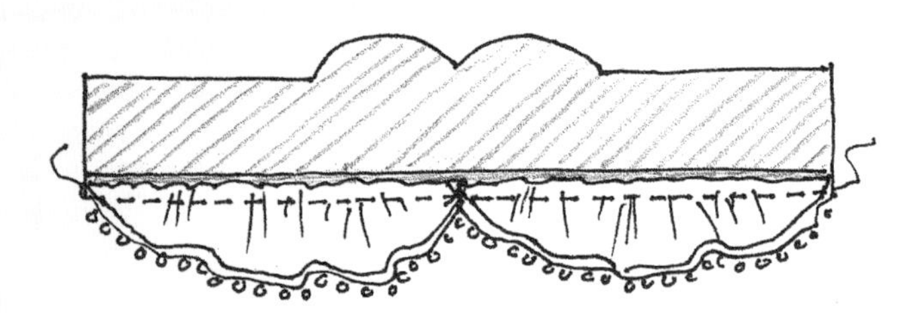

Figure 7

Figure 8

Here's a Hint

This outfit is made from shiny fabrics for a shimmery fishlike look. Be sure to follow the guidelines in the Sewing With Fancy Fabrics section to insure good results. The top has an extra layer to make it irides-cent, but can be eliminated to make construction easier. If desired, add straps to the top. Try stringing tiny shells together to make a necklace or a bracelet for additional fun accessories.

Hair Clip Instructions

1 Cut the ribbon into three sections. Make a 1" (2.5cm) loop and insert a hand stitching needle with thread. Don't pull the needle through the ribbon yet. Make four to five more loops, varying the size, and place them on the needle. Pull the thread tightly through the ribbon and secure with a few stitches. Repeat with the remaining ribbons. (Figure 9)

2 Glue the ribbons to the barrette with the loops toward the outside. (Figure 10) Glue a shell over the center of the loops. (Figure 11)

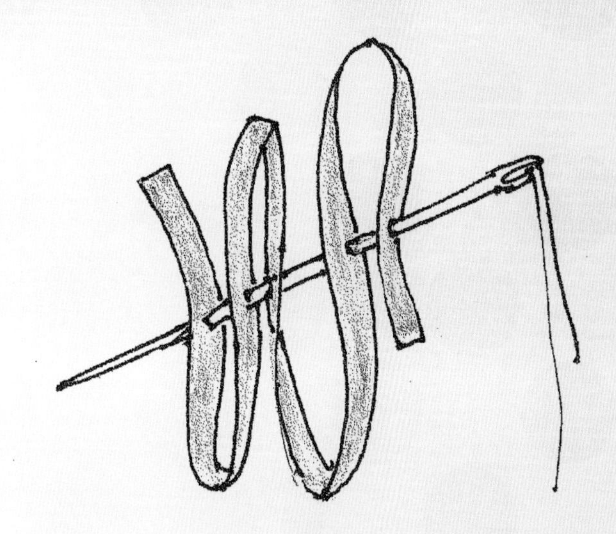

Figure 9

Figure 10

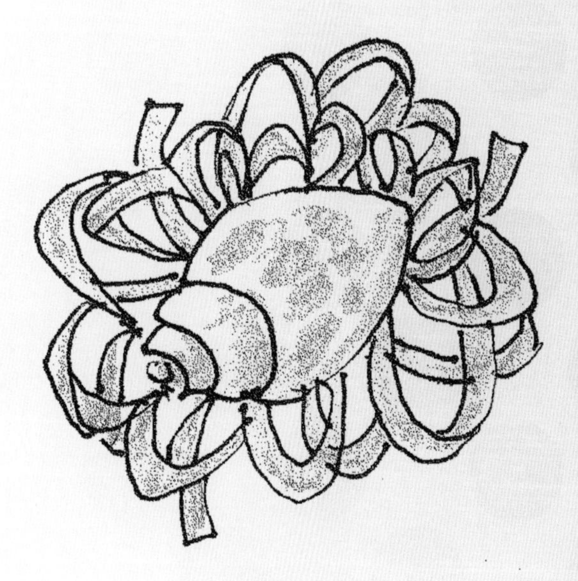

Figure 11

Playtime

Cowgirl

Shirt, Skirt, Vest, Scarf and Belt

Your doll is sure to win first prize at the local rodeo with her lively cowgirl outfit. The cow print full skirt and vest are trimmed with pink fringe. The blouse can be worn with a pair of jeans or other clothing, too. Add a sparkly belt buckle using a piece of repurposed jewelry. With matching hat and boots, this cowgirl's ready to kick up her heels.

Shirt Supplies

Cowgirl pattern pieces: Shirt Front, Shirt Back, Shirt Sleeve, Shirt Collar

¼ yard (0.2m) white cotton fabric

3 buttons, size ¼" (6mm)

3 snaps

Vest and Skirt Supplies

Cowgirl pattern pieces: Vest

⅓ yard (0.3m) cow print cotton fabric

1½ yard (1.4m) of fringe trim, 1¼" (3.2cm) wide

11" (27.9cm) elastic, ¼" (6mm) wide

Scarf Supplies

Cowgirl pattern pieces: Scarf

¼ yard (0.2m) print fabric

Belt Supplies

13½" (34.3cm) of grosgrain ribbon, ⅞" (22mm) wide

1" (2.5cm) strip of hook and loop tape

jewelry finding to resemble belt buckle, size 1" (2.5cm)

Shirt Instructions

1 Cut four fronts, two backs, two sleeves and one collar. Cut two 2" × 5" (5.1cm × 12.7cm) cuffs from the white fabric.

2 With right sides together, sew two fronts to one back at the shoulder seams. Repeat with the other fronts and back to make a lining. (Figure 1) Press the seam allowances open.

3 With right sides together, fold the collar in half lengthwise. Mark the center point. Stitch across the short ends. (Figure 2) Clip the corners, turn to the right side and press.

4 With right sides together, center the collar along the neckline of the shirt. Match the center points. The collar does not go all the way to the center front edges. Stitch in place. (Figure 3)

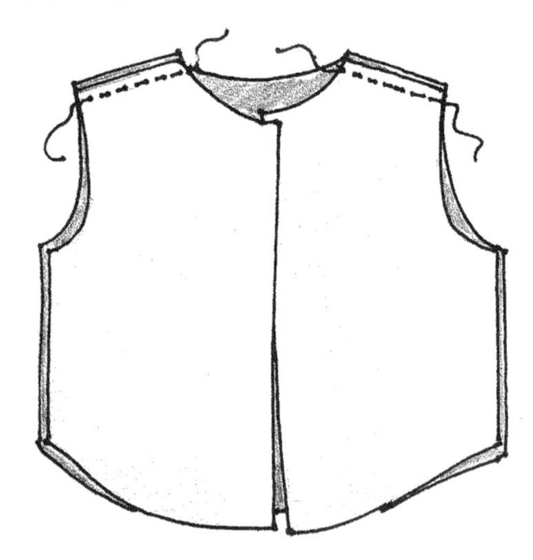

Figure 1

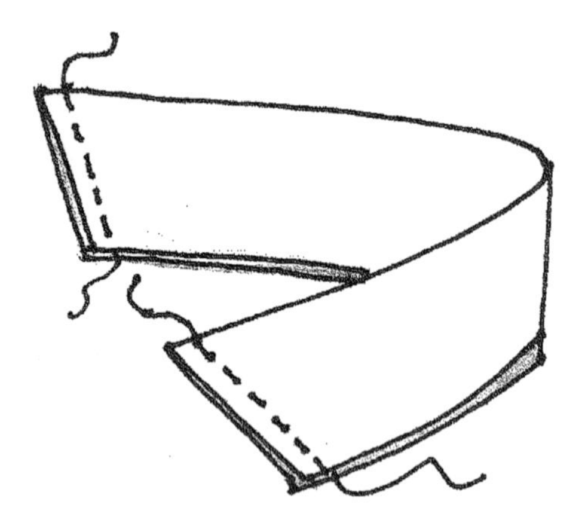

Figure 2

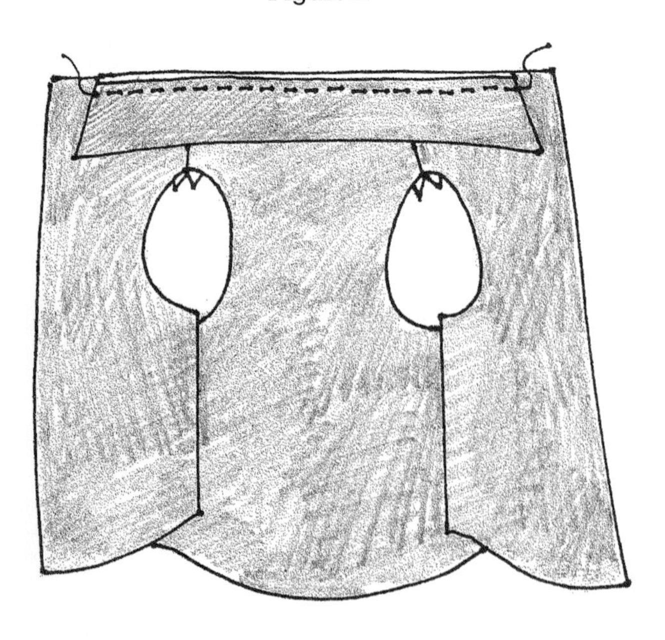

Figure 3

5 With right sides together, pin the shirt lining to the shirt, sandwiching the collar in between. Sew around the neckline and down the center fronts. (Figure 4) Clip the curves, turn to the right side, and press.

6 Press one long edge of each cuff ¼" (6mm) to the wrong side. With the right side of the cuff to the wrong side of the sleeve, sew along the unpressed edge. Sew the right side of the other long edge to the wrong side of the sleeve. (Figure 5) Fold the cuff over the stitching line and stitch in place.

7 Gather the sleeve caps between the marks. Sew the sleeves to the armholes, easing in the sleeves.

8 Sew the underarm seams from the cuff to the bottom of the shirt.

9 Serge or zigzag stitch the lower edge of the shirt. (Figure 6) Press the edge ¼" (6mm) to the wrong side and topstitch.

10 Lapping right over left, sew the buttons to the right front, placing the first one at the neck edge and the rest 1" (2.5cm) apart. Sew the snaps under the buttons.

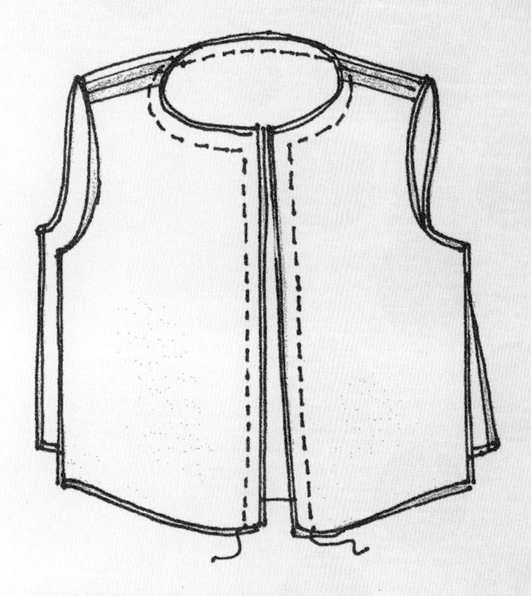

Figure 4

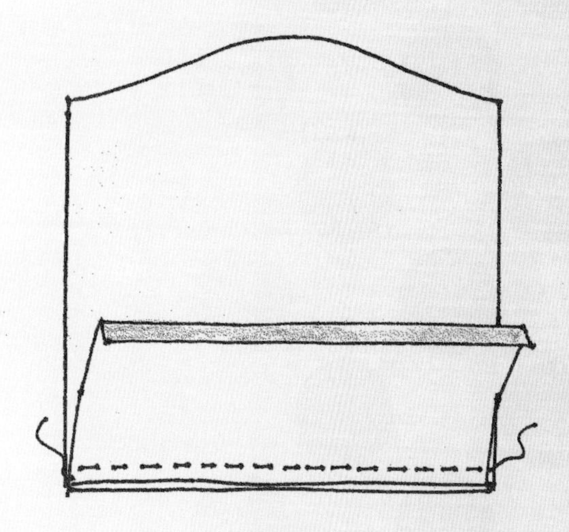

Figure 5

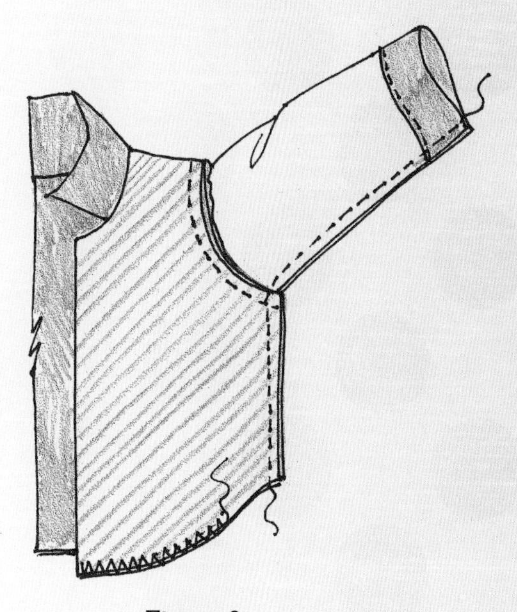

Figure 6

Skirt Instructions

1 Cut one 5½" × 40" (14cm × 101.6cm) rectangle for the skirt from the cow print fabric.

2 Serge or zigzag along both long sides of the skirt piece. Stitch the heading of the fringe trim to one serged edge over the previous stitching. (Figure 7)

3 Fold the opposite edge ¾" (19mm) to the wrong side and press. Stitch ½" (13mm) from the pressed edge to create a casing at the waist. Thread elastic through the casing and secure the ends. With right sides together, sew the short edges together and press. (Figure 8)

Vest Instructions

1 Cut two vests from the cow print fabric. (One will be used for the lining.) Press the shoulder seams of the lining ¼" (6mm) to the wrong side.

2 With right sides together, sew the vest to the lining around all outside edges but not across the shoulder seams, leaving a 2" (5.1cm) opening at the center bottom for turning. (Figure 9) Clip the curves, turn to the right side and press.

3 Sew the shoulder seams of the vest only, being careful not to catch the lining. Tuck the shoulder seams under the folds of the lining and slipstitch closed.

4 On the right side, place the heading of the fringe trim over the lower edge of the vest and stitch, folding in the raw edges of the trim ¼" (6mm). (Figure 10)

Figure 7

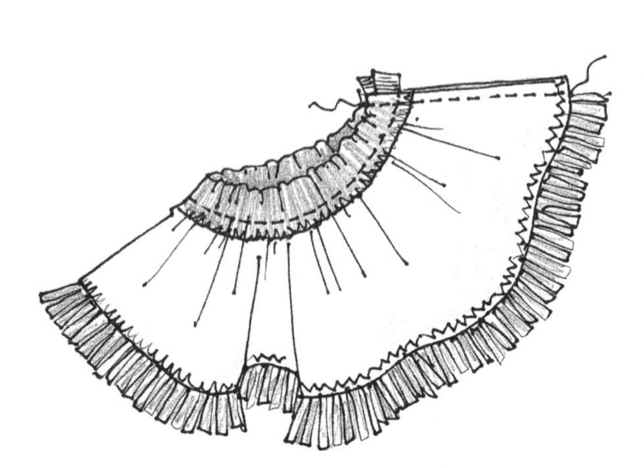

Figure 8

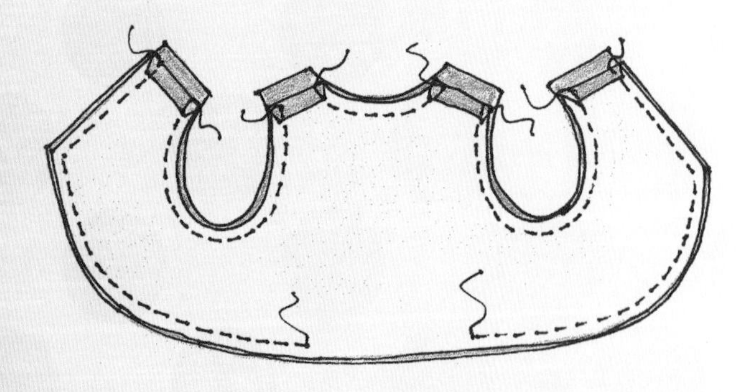

Figure 9

Figure 10

Scarf Instructions

1 Cut one scarf from the print fabric.

2 Serge or zigzag all edges of the scarf. Press the edges ¼" (6mm) to the wrong side, folding in the tips of the scarf to the wrong side. Topstitch all of the edges. (Figure 11)

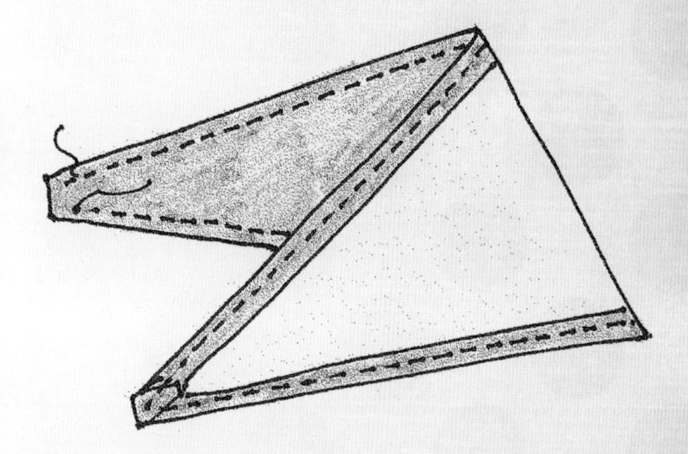

Figure 11

Belt Instructions

1 Fold back one end of the ribbon ½" (13mm) to the wrong side. Stitch the hook side of the hook and loop tape to this end.

2 Fold the other end of the ribbon ½" (13mm) to the right side. Stitch the loop side of the hook and loop tape to this end.

3 Sew the jewelry finding to the center of the belt. (Figure 12)

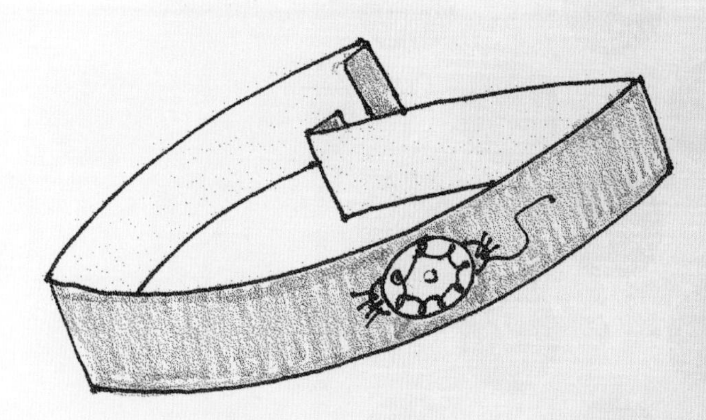

Figure 12

Here's a Hint

To make this outfit extra easy, the button-down shirt can be replaced with a purchased T-shirt or turtleneck. You can decorate your cowgirl's hat and boots with lots of rhinestone trims and colorful ribbons. Find a small "sheriff" badge at party stores for a boost of Wild West authority!

Superhero

Top, Skirt, Belt and Cape

Your doll will surely be able to leap tall buildings in her *Superhero* costume. The top and circle skirt are made from satin, but cottons could be substituted. A purchased appliqué star is fused to the front of the top, making the garment quick and easy. The lined cape is attached with snaps to the top. Finish the look off with white boots—the perfect footwear for chasing the bad guys!

Top, Skirt and Belt Supplies

- *Superhero* pattern pieces: Belt, Skirt, Top Front, Top Back
- ⅓ yard (0.3m) blue satin fabric
- ¼ yard (0.2m) red fabric (lining and belt)
- 3" (7.6cm) strip of hook and loop tape, cut in half (top)
- 1 iron-on appliqué star, about 1" (2.5cm)
- 1 hook and eye
- 3" × 14" (7.6cm × 35.6cm) lightweight fusible interfacing
- 1" (2.5cm) strip of hook and loop tape (belt)

Cape Supplies

- (2) 10" × 10" (25.4cm × 25.4cm) pieces of red star fabric (cape)
- 6½" (16.5cm) single-fold bias tape
- 2 snaps

Top Instructions

1 Cut one front and two backs from the blue fabric, and one front and two backs from the lining fabric. With right sides together, sew the shoulder seams of the blue set and the lining set. Press seam allowances open.

2 With the blue set and the lining set right sides together, sew up the center back, around the neckline, down the other center back and around each armhole. (Figure 1) Clip the curves and corners, turn to the right side and press.

3 Open out through sides and press. Stitch the side seams with right sides together. (Figure 2)

4 Press the lower edges of the top ¼" (6mm) to the wrong side. Stitch the top and the lining together along the pressed edges. (Figure 3)

5 Lapping right over left, sew hook and loop tape to the back opening.

6 Fuse the star to the center of the top about ¾" (19mm) down from the neckline.

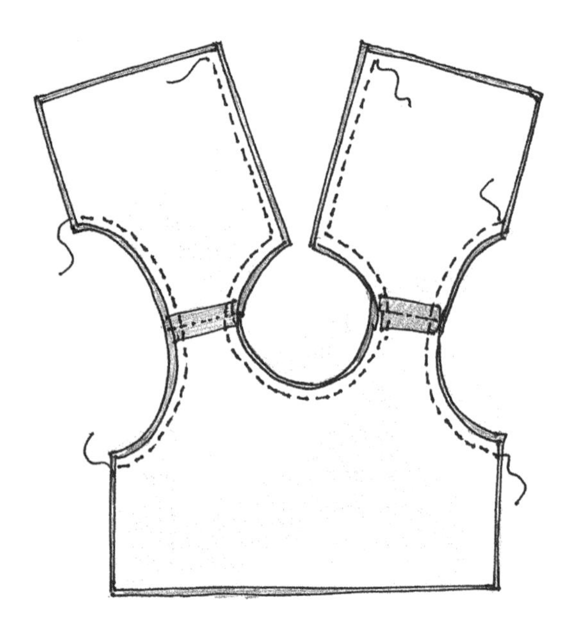

Figure 1

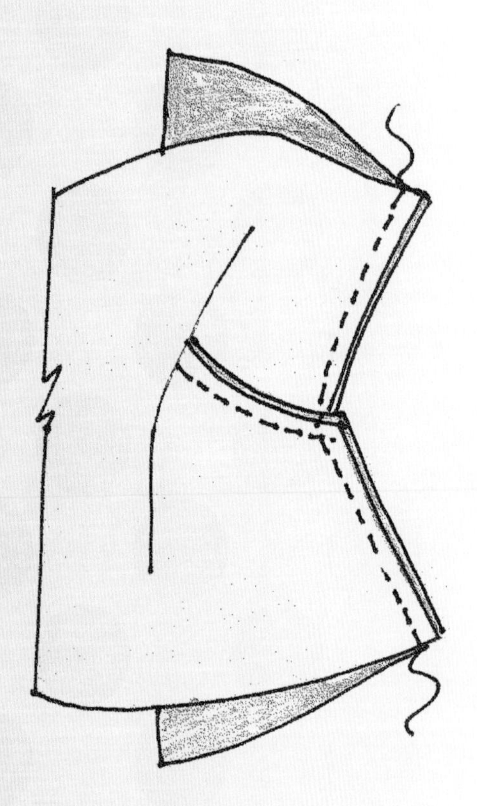

Figure 2

Figure 3

Skirt Instructions

1 Cut one front skirt, two back skirts and a 1½" × 12½" (3.8cm × 31.8cm) waistband.

2 Serge or zigzag each center back seam separately. Sew the center back seam from the dot marked on the pattern piece to the lower edge of the skirt. Press the seam allowances open, including the unstitched part of the seam. Topstitch along the pressed edges.

3 With right sides together, sew the side seams and press. (Figure 4)

4 Serge or zigzag around the lower edge. Press this edge ¼" (6mm) to the wrong side and topstitch.

5 Press one long edge of the waistband ¼" (6mm) to the wrong side. Pin the opposite edge of the waistband to the wrong side of the skirt, extending the right short end by ¼" (6mm) and the left end by ½" (13mm); stitch. Fold the waistband over to the right side and stitch in place, tucking in the short ends. (Figure 5)

6 Stitch a snap or hook and eye to the waistband overlapping the short end over the long one.

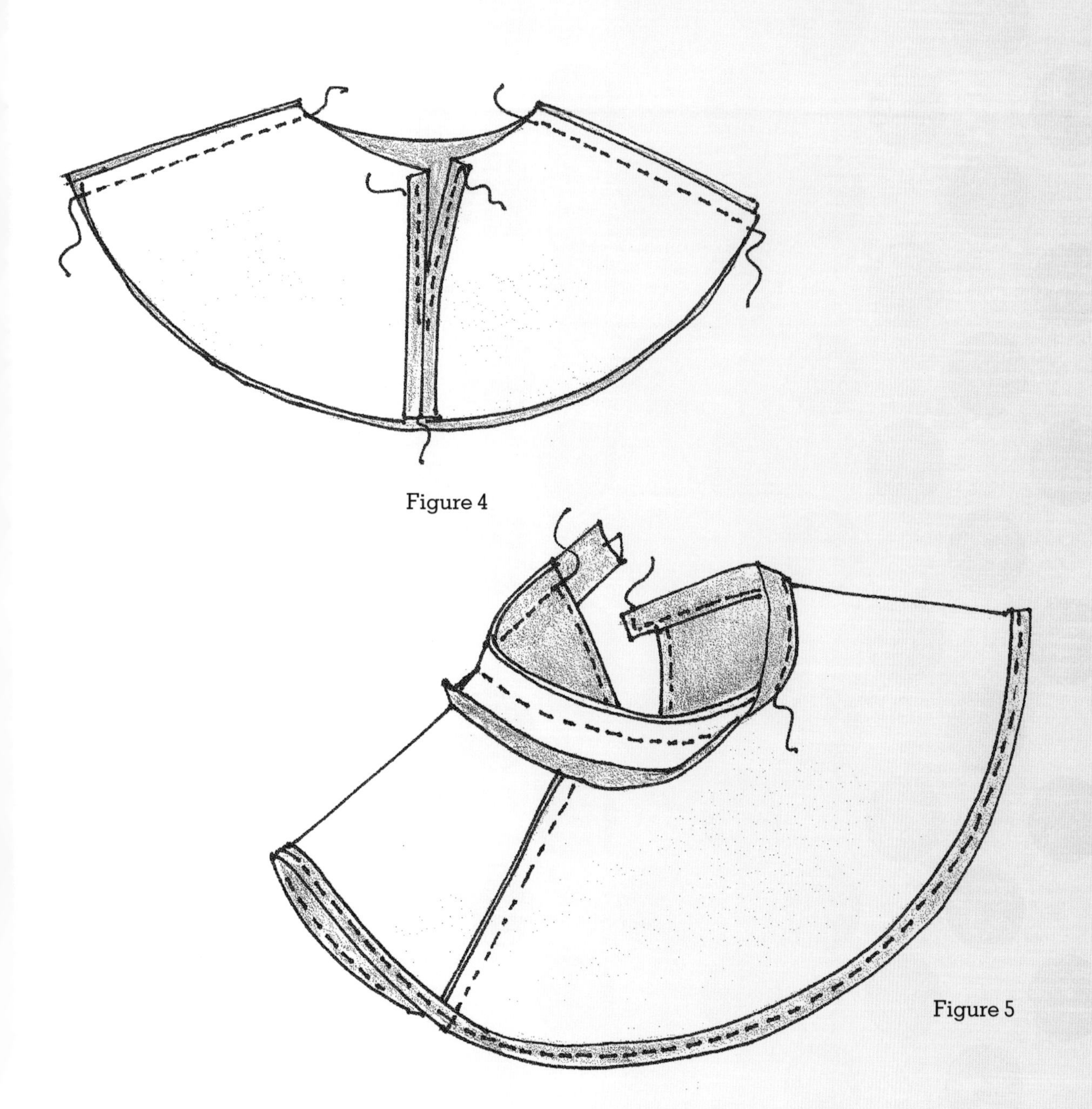

Figure 4

Figure 5

Belt Instructions

1 Fuse interfacing to the wrong side of the red fabric following the manufacturer's instructions. Cut one belt piece from the fabric and one from the fabric with interfacing. (Figure 6)

2 With right sides together, sew the belts along the long sides and one short end. (Figure 7) Clip the curves, turn to the right side and press. Fold the raw edges of the unsewn end ¼" (6mm) to the wrong side and topstitch.

3 Sew hook and loop tape to the ends of the belt.

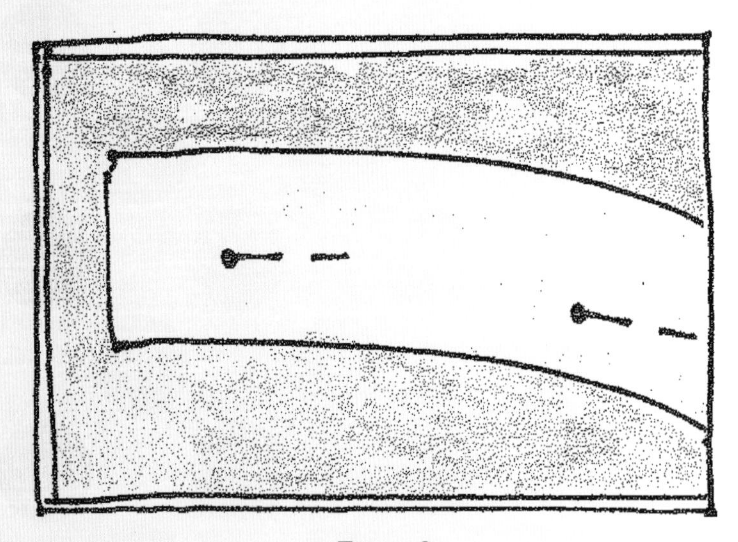

Figure 6

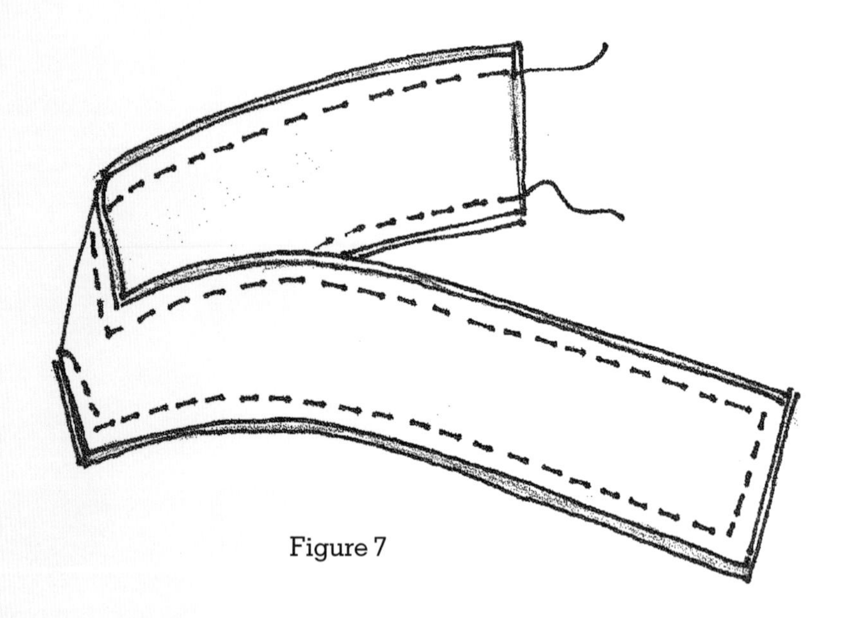

Figure 7

Cape Instructions

1 With right sides together, sew the cape pieces together along three sides. Turn to the right side and press.

2 Gather the top raw edges so that the cape measures 5½" (14cm) wide. Unfold the bias tape and sew the right side of the bias tape to the underside of the cape with ½" (13mm) extra tape on each end. Fold the tape to the right side and stitch in place. Bring the raw ends to the wrong side and stitch one half of a snap to each end. (The raw ends will be covered.) (Figure 8) Sew the other half of each snap to the top, ¼" (6mm) from the armholes on the shoulder seams.

Figure 8

Here's a Hint

While the star is the typical embellishment motif for superheroes of all types, the top can be embroidered with any design you choose. Perhaps a heart or initial will appeal more to your child. Be sure to embroider the design on the fabric before cutting out the top front. Don't forget to make a cape for your child to match her doll for more play time fun!

Playtime

Pilgrim

Blouse, Skirt, Collar, Cap and Apron

Relive the historic First Thanksgiving with this realistic *Pilgrim* costume. The blouse has a lined detachable collar, the skirt is covered by a simple apron and her cap ties underneath her chin. Bias tape makes for easy assembly. Don't forget the pumpkin pie!

Pilgrim Costume Supplies

Pilgrim pattern pieces: Blouse Front, Blouse Back, Blouse Sleeve, Collar Front, Collar Back, Cap

½ yard (0.5m) brown cotton fabric

½ yard (0.5m) white cotton fabric

2½" (6.4cm) strip of hook and loop tape, cut in half

12½" (31.8cm) brown single-fold bias tape, ⅞" (22mm) wide

1 hook and eye

21" (53.3cm) white single-fold bias tape, ½" (13mm) wide

1 medium snap

⅔ yard (0.6m) white satin ribbon, ½" (13mm) wide

32" (81.03cm) white grosgrain ribbon, ⅝" (16mm) wide

Blouse Instructions

1 Cut two fronts, four backs and two sleeves from the brown fabric. Cut two 2½" × 6¼" (6.4cm × 15.9cm) cuffs from the white fabric.

2 With right sides together, sew one front to two backs at the shoulders. Press seam allowances open. Repeat with the remaining lining pieces. (Figure 1)

3 Sew the lining to the blouse up one center back, around the neckline and down the other center back. Stitch along the bottom edges of the front and the backs. (Figure 2) Clip the curves, turn right side out through the sides and press.

4 With wrong sides together, fold the cuffs in half widthwise to make them 1¼" (3cm) wide × 6¼" (15.9cm). Press. With the raw edge of the cuff placed on the wrong side of the sleeve edges, stitch the cuffs to the sleeves. Turn the cuff over to the right side of each sleeve. (Figure 3)

5 With right sides together, stitch the sleeves to the armholes. Press the seam allowances toward the sleeves. Sew the underarm seam, from the sleeve edge to the bottom of the blouse. (Figure 4)

6 Lapping right over left, sew hook and loop tape to the back opening.

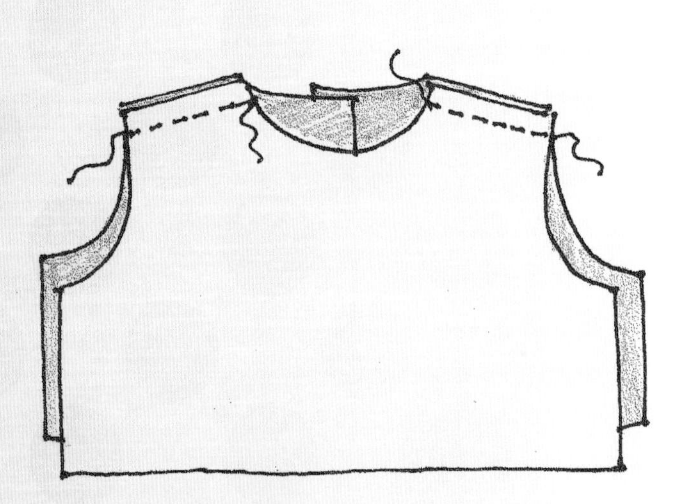

Figure 1

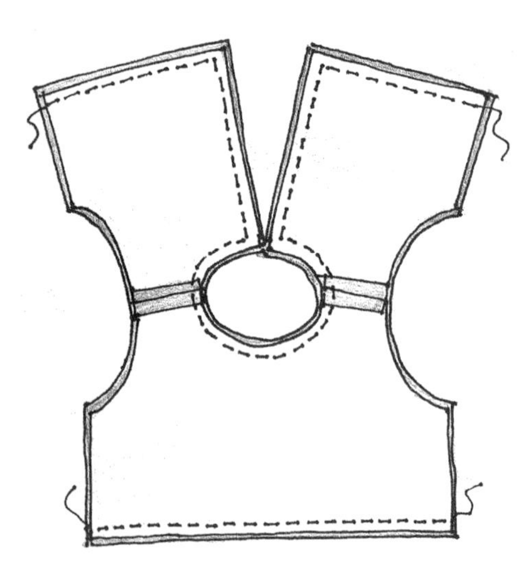

Figure 2

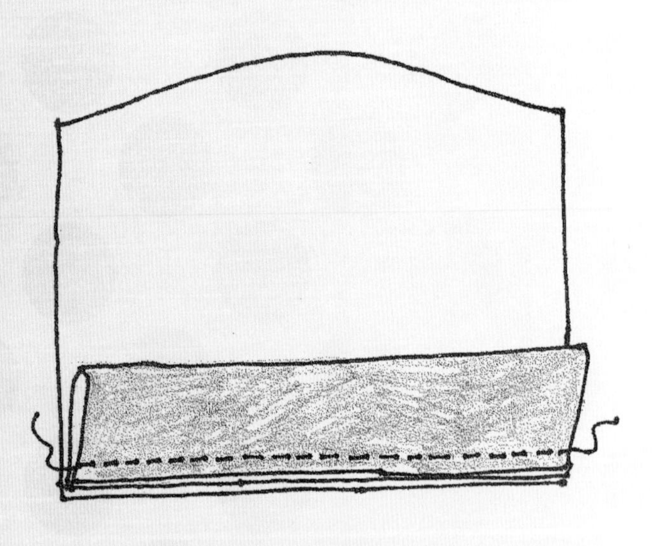

Figure 3

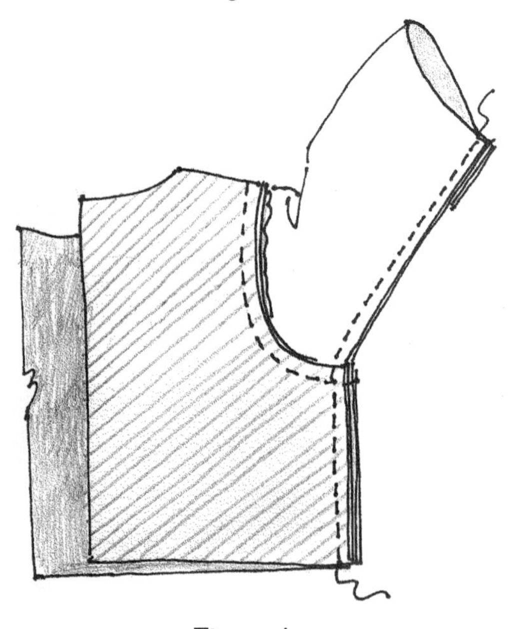

Figure 4

Skirt Instructions

1 Cut a 10" × 25" (25.4cm × 63.5cm) skirt piece from the brown fabric.

2 Serge or zigzag stitch the sides and bottom edge of the skirt. Press these edges ¼" (6mm) to the wrong side and stitch in place. (Figure 5)

3 Press the ends of the brown bias tape ¼" (6mm) to the wrong side. Then press the bias tape in half widthwise. Gather the top edge of the skirt until it is the same width as the bias tape. Place the top edge of the skirt inside of the bias tape so that the gathers are enclosed and stitch in place. Stitch the short ends. (Figure 6)

4 Lapping right over left, sew the hook and eye to the waistband.

Figure 5

Figure 6

Collar Instructions

1 Cut four fronts and two backs from the white cotton fabric.

2 With right sides together, sew the shoulder seams in two fronts and one back. Repeat with the remaining lining pieces. Press the seam allowances open.

3 Sew the collar to the lining along the center front, around the outer edge and along the other center front. (Figure 7) Clip the curves, turn to the right side and press.

4 Cut 9" (22.9cm) of white bias tape. Press the ends ¼" (6mm) to the wrong side. Press the bias tape in half widthwise. Enclose the neck edge of the collar inside the bias tape and stitch in place. The ends will extend a bit, enough for them to cross. Sew a snap on those tabs. (Figure 8)

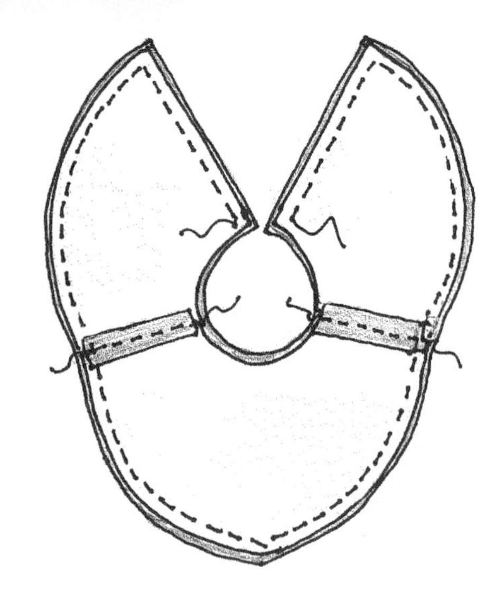

Figure 7

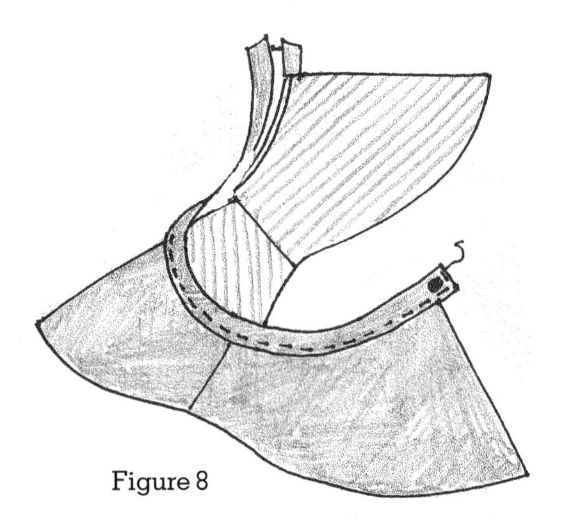

Figure 8

Here's a Hint

Make a doll-sized pumpkin pie for your doll. All you need is tan and red-orange polymer clay and a muffin tin. Roll the tan clay into a 6" (15.2cm) circle to fit the tin and trim the excess. Press enough red-orange clay into the tin to make the filling. Make a twisted rope from the tan clay to go around the edge of the pie. Following the manufacturer's instructions, bake to harden and serve with pride.

Cap Instructions

1 Cut one cap and a 4" × 10" (10.2cm × 25.4cm) band from the white fabric.

2 Sew gathering stitches along the curved edge of the cap and set aside.

3 With right sides together, fold the band in half widthwise and stitch the short ends. Turn to the right side and press. Pin the raw edges of the band to the wrong side of the cap along the straight edge. Stitch in place. Press the band to the right side. (Figure 9)

4 Pull the gathers of the cap so that it measures 11½" (29.2cm). Press the remainder of the bias tape in half widthwise. Enclose the gathered edge inside the bias tape and stitch, tucking in the short ends.

5 Cut the white satin ribbon in half. Fold one end ½" (13mm) to the wrong side and stitch at an angle to the side of the cap over the brim. Repeat with the other side. (Figure 10)

Apron Instructions

1 Cut a 10" × 20" (25.4cm × 50.8cm) apron from the white fabric. With right sides together, fold the apron in half to make a 10" (25.4cm) square.

2 Stitch along the two open sides and turn to the right side. (Figure 11) Press.

3 Gather the top edges together so that the apron measures 5" (12.7cm) wide. Center grosgrain ribbon over the gathers and topstitch. (Figure 12)

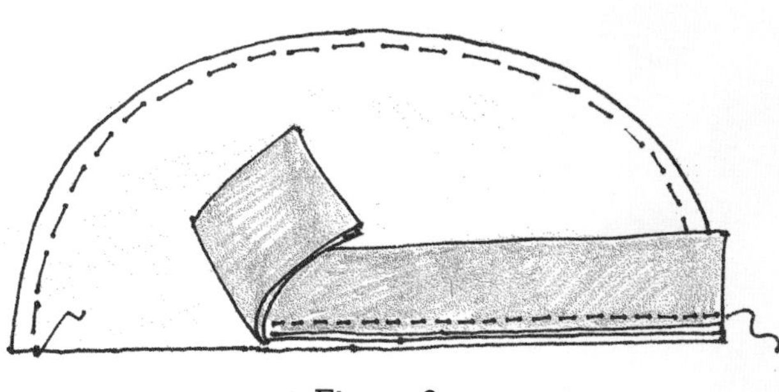

Figure 9

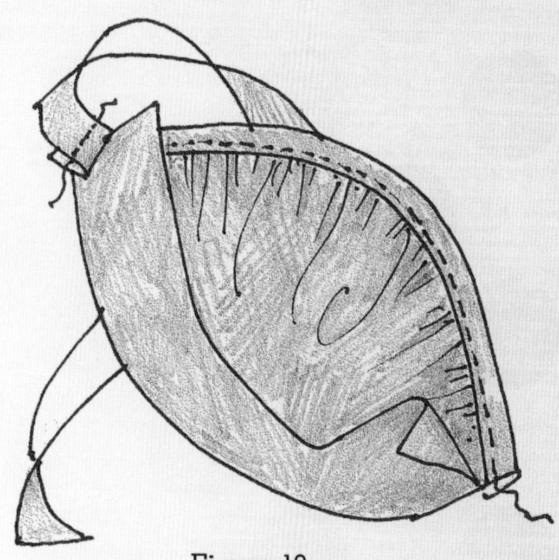

Figure 10

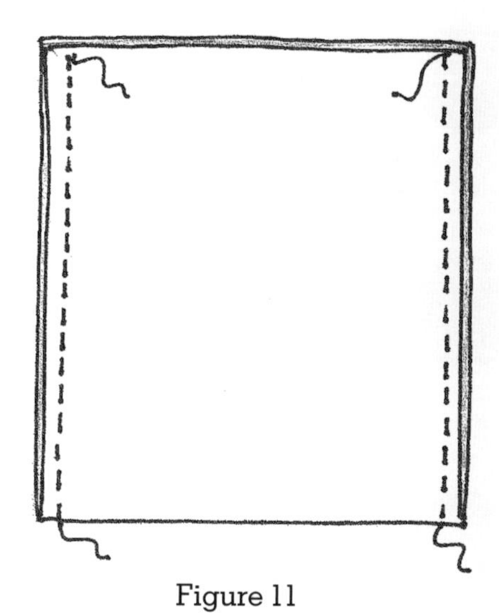

Figure 11

Figure 12

Playtime

Sock Hop Dancer

Poodle Skirt and Knit Shirt

The poodle skirt is the iconic wardrobe essential from the 1950s. This doll-sized version is quick and easy to make for any dress-up occasion. The skirt is made out of flannel, but if you make it from felt, you can eliminate the hem. The appliqué is ironed on with fusible web. To make the skirt even easier, glue the braid as well. Pair the skirt with a boat neck T-shirt with tiny pearl buttons and a chiffon scarf to finish the look.

Poodle Skirt Supplies

- *Sock Hop Dancer* pattern pieces: Skirt, Poodle, Poodle Ear
- ⅓ yard (0.3m) flannel or felt fabric
- scrap of white felt
- 15–20 black beads
- 8" (20.3cm) soutache braid
- 2 pompoms, size ½" (13mm)
- scrap of paper-backed fusible web
- beading needle and thread
- hand sewing needle
- snap or hook and eye
- fabric glue

Boat Neck T-Shirt Supplies

- *Sock Hop Dancer* pattern pieces: Boatneck T-Shirt Front, Boatneck T-Shirt Back, Boatneck T-Shirt Sleeve
- ¼ yard (0.2m) knit fabric
- 3 pearl shank buttons, size ¼" (6mm)
- 3" (7.6cm) strip of hook and loop tape

Scarf Supplies

- 5" × 20" (12.7cm × 51cm) piece of chiffon fabric

Poodle Skirt Instructions

1 Cut out one front and two backs from the fabric. Transfer pattern marks. Cut a 1½" × 12½" (3.8cm × 38.1cm) rectangle for the waistband.

2 If using flannel, serge or zigzag stitch each center back seam separately. Sew the center back seam from the dot marked on the pattern piece to the lower edge of the skirt. Press the seam allowances open, including the unstitched part of the seam. Topstitch along the pressed edges.

3 With right sides together, sew the side seams and press.

4 Serge or zigzag stitch around the lower edge of the skirt. (Figure 1) Then press the edge ¼" (6mm) to the wrong side and topstitch in place. (Figure 2)

5 Apply the fusible web to the white felt, following the manufacturer's instructions. Cut out the poodle and the ear. Remove the paper backing and fuse the poodle to the lower left front of the skirt, as shown on the pattern piece. Fuse the ear to the top of the poodle where indicated.

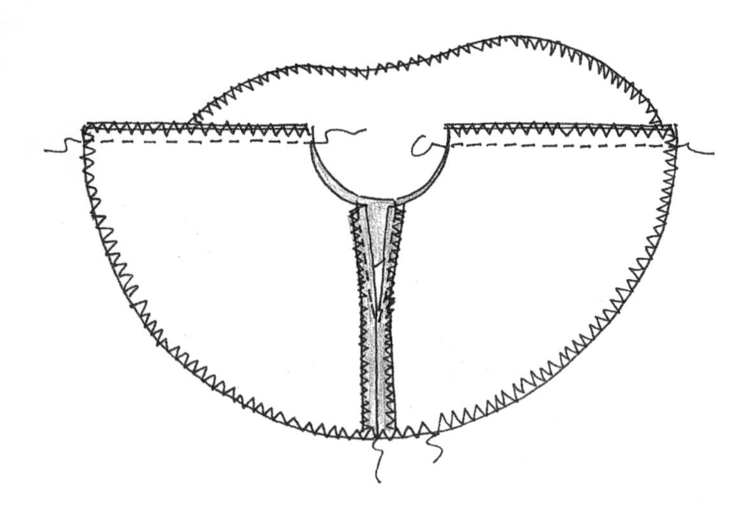

Figure 1

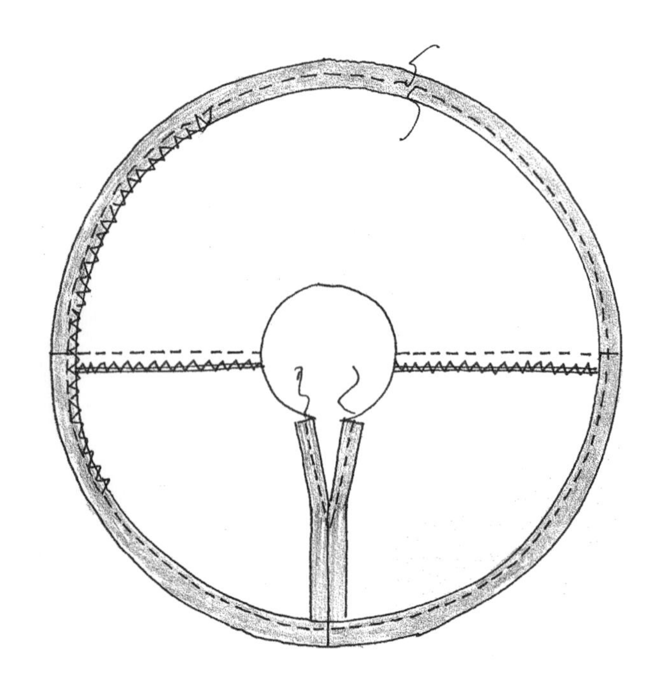

Figure 2

6 Using a straight stitch, stitch the soutache braid to the skirt as shown on the pattern piece, tucking one end slightly under the poodle at the neck. With a beading needle and thread, hand-stitch beads across the poodle's neck to make a collar. Stitch on one bead for the eye. Glue a pompom to the top of the head and to the top of the tail. (You may have to clip the pompom with scissors to give it the desired shape.) (Figure 3)

7 Press one long edge and the two short ends of the waistband ¼" (6mm) to the wrong side. Pin the other long edge of the waistband to the wrong side of the skirt, extending the right end by ¼" (6mm) and the left end by ½" (13mm) beyond the opening. Stitch the waistband to the skirt. Press the seam toward the waistband. (Figure 4) Fold the waistband to the right side and top stitch.

8 Stitch a snap or hook and eye to the waistband.

Figure 3

Figure 4

Boat Neck T-Shirt Instructions

1 Cut one front, two backs and two sleeves from the knit fabric.

2 With right sides together, sew the shoulder seams and press the seams open. Press each center back ¼" (6mm) to the wrong side and stitch in place. (Figure 5)

3 Press the neckline ¼" (6mm) to the wrong side and stitch in place.

4 Press the lower edge of each sleeve to the wrong side and stitch in place. (Figure 6)

5 With right sides together, sew the sleeve caps to the armholes, easing as necessary. Sew the underarm and side seam. (Figure 7)

6 Press the lower edge of the shirt ¼" (6mm) to the wrong side and stitch in place.

7 Lapping the right back over left back, sew the hook and loop tape to the back opening.

8 Sew the buttons to the center front of the shirt approximately ½" (13mm) apart.

Figure 5

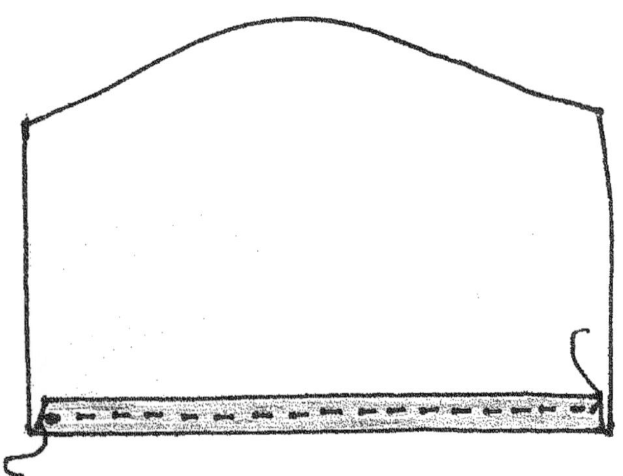

Figure 6

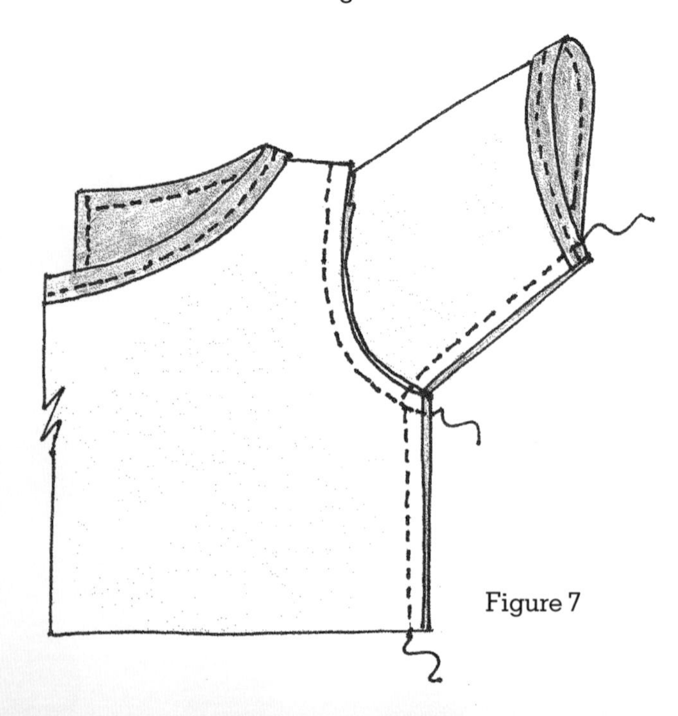

Figure 7

Scarf Instructions

1 Fold the fabric in half lengthwise with right sides together. Sew the long edge and one of the short ends. (Figure 8) Trim the seam allowances, turn to the right side and press.

2 Fold the open end ¼" (6mm) to the inside and topstitch.

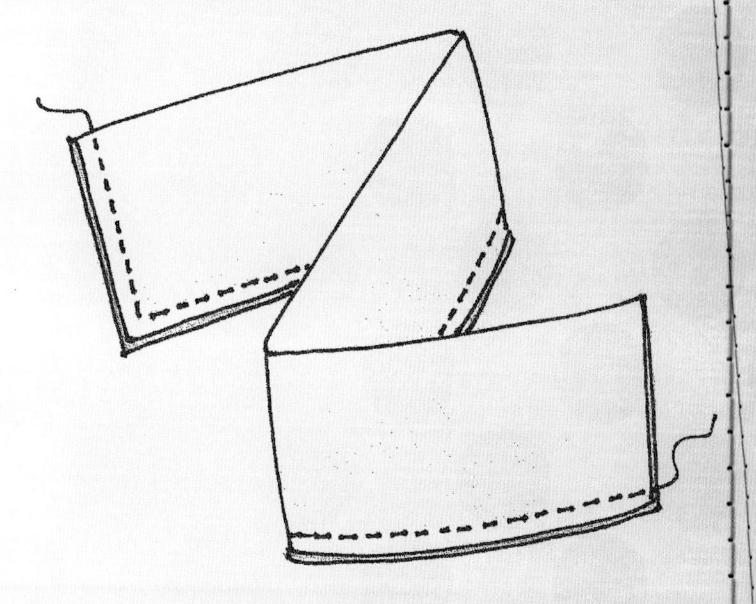

Figure 8

Here's a Hint

Try making the skirt with different kinds of appliqués. To be authentic, the poodle can be replaced with a black record or music notes. For more modern occasions, use holiday appliqués such as Christmas trees or ornaments hanging from a cord. Pair the skirt with a purchased sweater instead of the knit shirt.

Ladybug

Turtleneck, Footless Tights, Ladybug Body, Wings and Antennae

Your doll will be as cute as a bug when she wears this fun *Ladybug* costume. The pattern pieces are the same for the *Pumpkin* costume. Substitute red and black polka-dot fabric for the body and eliminate the pumpkin face. The wings are simply wire stitched onto netting and then cut out. The antennae are applied to a purchased headband, but you can make your own headband from chenille stems following the directions in the *Kitty Cat* costume.

Turtleneck, Tights and Ladybug Body Supplies

Ladybug pattern pieces: Turtleneck Front, Turtleneck Back, Turtleneck Sleeve, Footless Tights, Costume Front, Costume Back

⅓ yard (0.3m) black knit fabric (must have two-way stretch)

21" (53.3cm) elastic, ½" (13mm) wide

3" (7.6cm) strip of hook and loop tape (turtleneck), cut lengthwise

⅓ yard (0.3m) red and black polka-dot cotton fabric

1 snap

Wings and Antennae Supplies

Ladybug pattern pieces: Wing

¼ yard (0.2m) black netting

1 yard (0.9m) of 30-gauge covered wire

chalk pencil

purchased black headband

2 black chenille stems, 4" (10.2cm) long

2 red pompoms, size 1" (2.5cm)

fabric glue

Turtleneck and Footless Tights Instructions

Follow the instructions for the *Pumpkin* costume.

Ladybug Body Instructions

Follow the instructions for the *Pumpkin* body, eliminating the pumpkin face in step 4.

Wings Instructions

1 Fold the netting so you have four layers. Trace the wing shape on the netting with the chalk pencil. Begin stitching wire over the pattern outline at one of the corners using a narrow zigzag stitch. Follow the outline around the wing. (Figure 1) Cut out the wing close to the wire without clipping the stitching.

2 Flip the pattern over and repeat for the other wing.

3 Attach the wings to the back of the Ladybug body 1" (2.5cm) below the top edge and ½" (13mm) from the center back opening, using a zigzag stitch over the wire. (Figure 2)

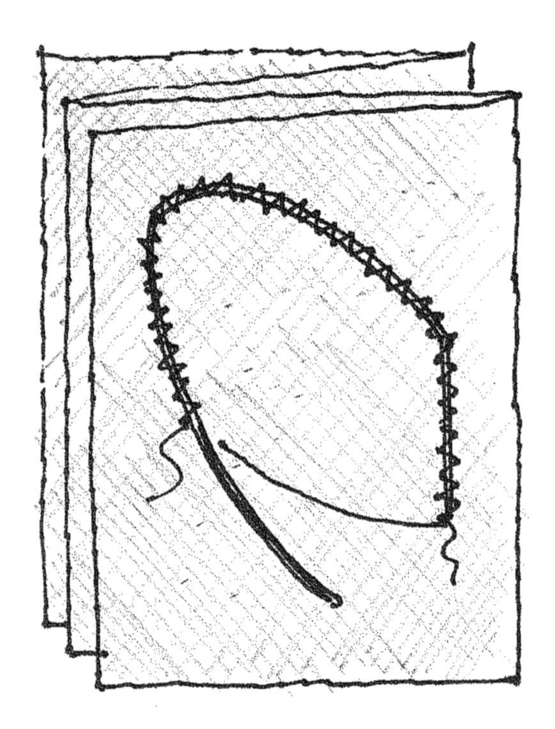

Figure 1

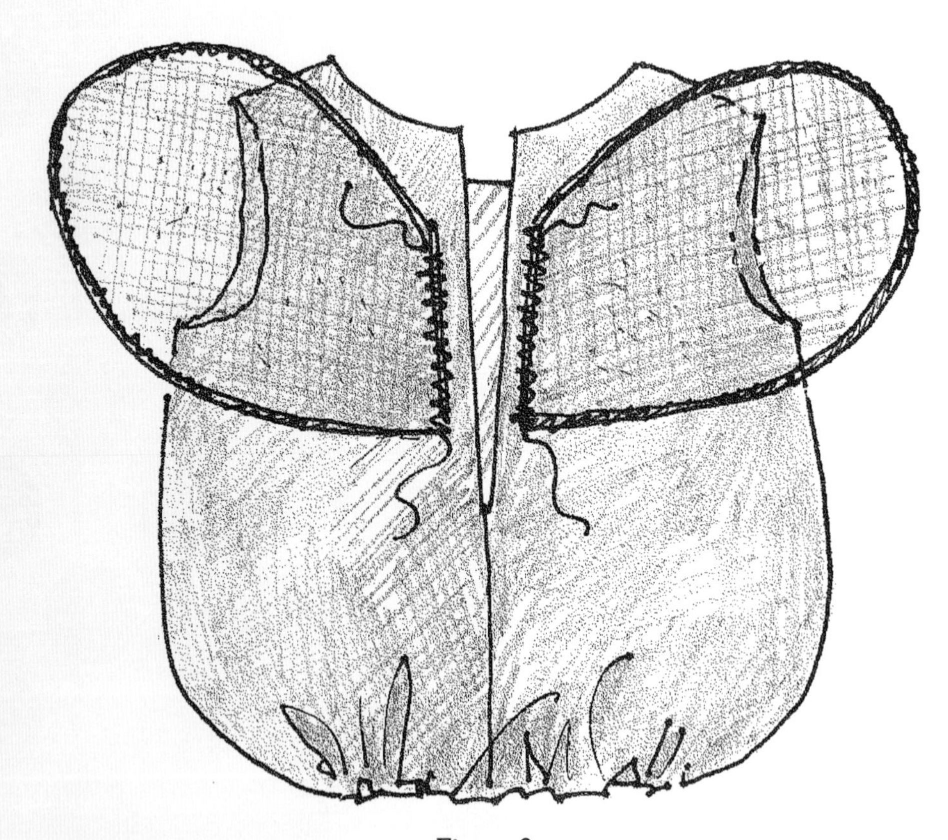

Figure 2

Antennae Instructions

1 Fold the ends of the chenille stems over the headband and twist the wire.

2 Glue the pompoms to each end. (Figure 3)

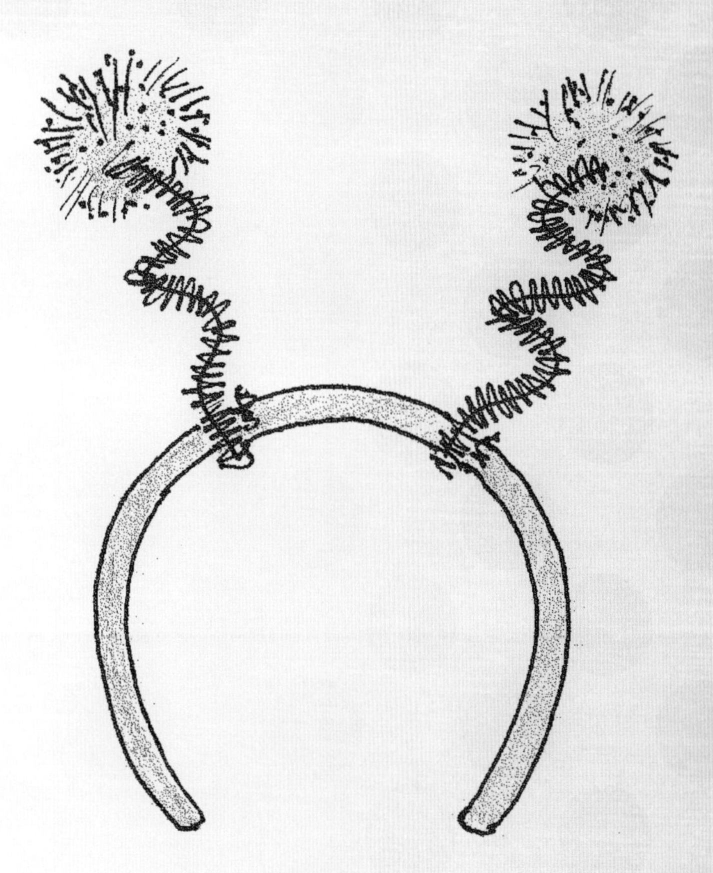

Figure 3

Here's a Hint

This pattern can also make an adorable bumblebee costume. Substitute the polka-dot fabric for yellow and black striped fabric. Bumblebee wings should be white rather than black. Change the color of the pompoms on the antennae to yellow and there you have it!

Doctor Scrubs

Top, Pants, Cap and Mask

Your doll will have the latest in medical professional attire with this ensemble! The top can be made from the whimsical novelty prints found in quilt shops. The placket may look tricky but is easy to do.

Top Supplies

Doctor pattern pieces: Top Front, Top Back, Top Sleeve, Placket

¼ yard (0.2m) print cotton fabric

4" (10.2cm) strip of hook and loop tape, cut in half

Pants and Cap Supplies

Doctor pattern pieces: Pants

½ yard (0.5m) cotton fabric

25" (63.5cm) elastic, ¼" (6mm) wide

Mask Supplies

2¾" × 8" (7cm × 20.3cm) piece of white fabric

60" (152.4cm) white single-fold bias tape

Top Instructions

1 Cut one front, two backs, two sleeves, four plackets and two 2" × 2" (5.1cm × 5.1cm) pockets from the print cotton fabric.

2 With right sides together, sew the shoulder seams of the front to the backs. Press seam allowances open. (Figure 1)

3 With right sides together, sew two of the plackets along the inner edge only. (Figure 2) Clip the curves, turn to the right side and press. Repeat with the other set.

4 With right sides together, pin one of plackets on the top's neckline. Match the center backs and stitch until you come to the *V* in the center front. On the top front, clip into the *V* with scissors. Repeat with the other placket. (Figure 3)

5 Press the plackets away from the top. With the left placket in front, fold the raw edges under by ¼" (6mm) so that the folded edge is flush with the seam line of the right placket. Pin the placket in place. Topstitch around the plackets on both sides of the placket/top seam line. Topstitch the center of the overlapped plackets to make a square.

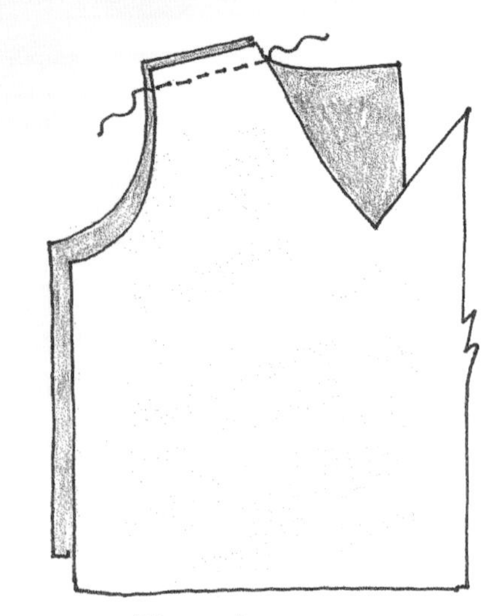

Figure 1

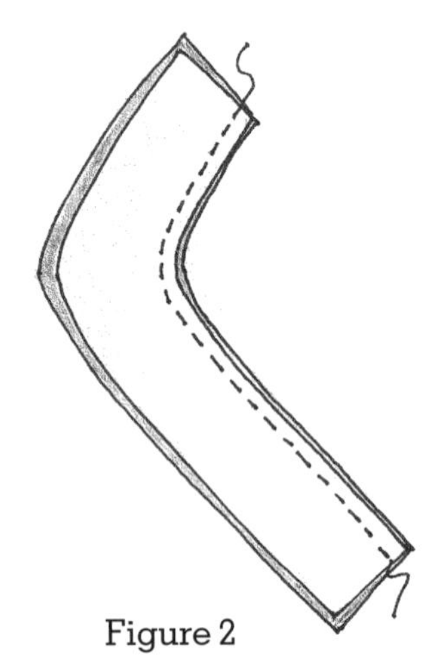

Figure 2

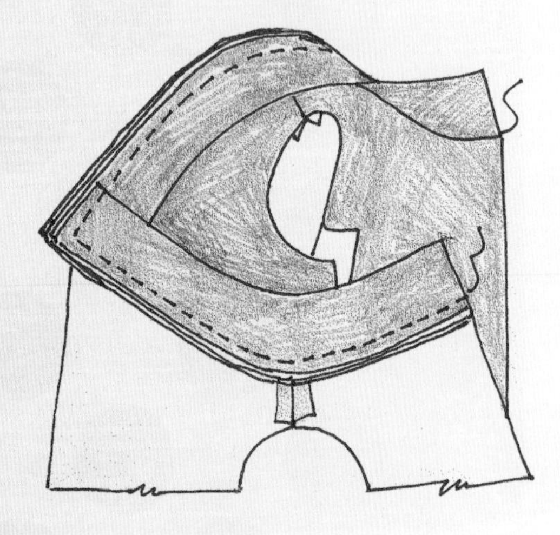

Figure 3

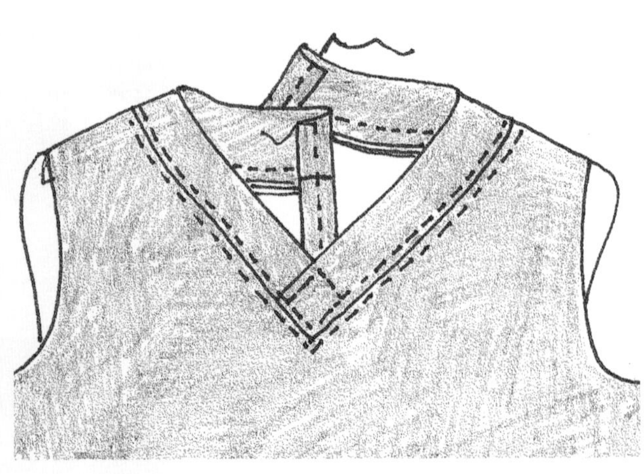

Figure 4

6 Serge or zigzag the center back edges. Press the center back edges, including the placket at the neckline, ¼" (6mm) to the wrong side. Stitch in place. (Figure 4)

7 Press all edges of the pockets ¼" (6mm) to the wrong side. Topstitch along one edge of each pocket to create the pocket top. (Figure 5)

Figure 5

8 Place each pocket on the top front 1½" (3.8cm) from the side edges and 1" (2.5cm) from the bottom edge. Stitch along the remaining three sides to attach the pockets to the top front. (Figure 6)

9 Serge or zigzag the lower edge of each sleeve. Press this edge ⅜" (10mm) to the wrong side and stitch. Gather the sleeve caps slightly to fit the armholes. With right sides together, sew the sleeves to the armholes. Press the seam allowances toward the sleeves.

Figure 6

10 With right sides together, sew the underarm seam from the sleeve edge to the lower edge of the top. (Figure 7)

11 Serge or zigzag the lower edge. Press in ⅜" (10mm) to the wrong side and stitch.

12 Lapping right over left, sew hook and loop tape to the back opening.

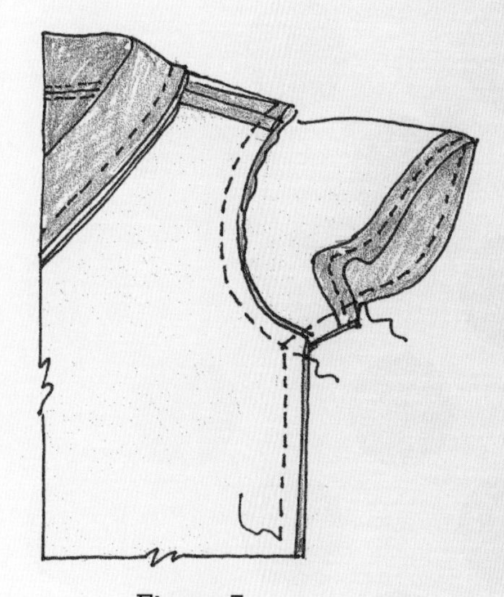

Figure 7

Pants Instructions

1 Cut four pants from the fabric.

2 With right sides together, sew the side seams of two of the pants pieces. Repeat with the remaining set and press. (Figure 7)

3 With right sides together, sew the center front seam and press.

4 Serge or zigzag stitch the top edge of the pants. Press this edge ¾" (19mm) to the wrong side and stitch ½" (13mm) from the fold to make a casing. Thread 11" (27.9cm) of elastic through the casing and secure both ends. With right sides together, sew the center back seam and press. (Figure 8)

5 Serge or zigzag the lower edges of each pant leg. Press ½" (13mm) to the wrong side and stitch. With right sides together, sew the inner leg seam. (Figure 9)

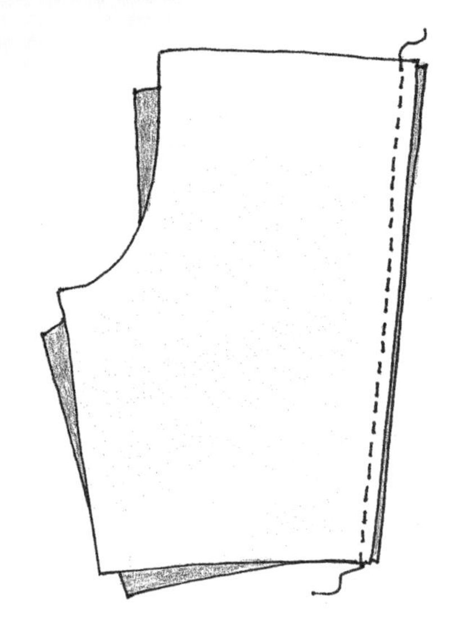

Figure 7

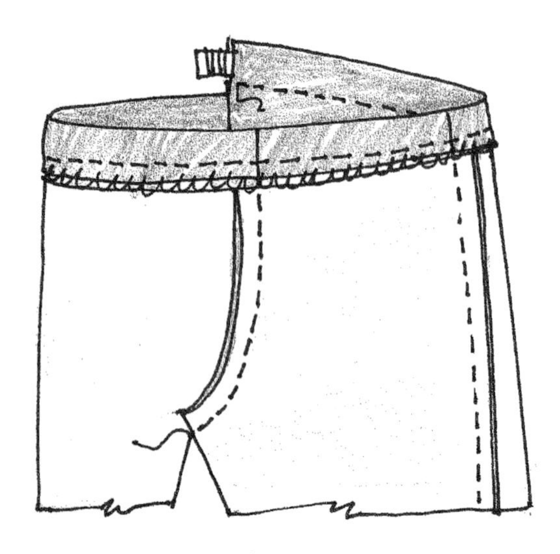

Figure 8

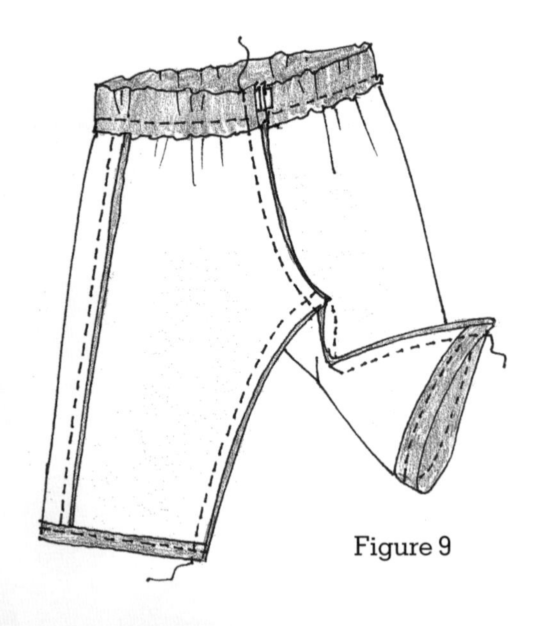

Figure 9

Cap Instructions

1 Cut a 13" (33cm) circle from the fabric using a dinner plate or other large circle for your guide.

2 Serge or zigzag the raw edge of the cap. Press the edge ½" (13mm) to the wrong side, overlapping the fabric as necessary to maintain the curve. (Figure 10)

3 Stitch ⅜" (10mm) from the edge, leaving a 1" (2.5cm) opening to insert the elastic. (Figure 10) Thread the remaining elastic through the casing and stitch the ends of the elastic together. Stitch the opening closed. (Figure 11)

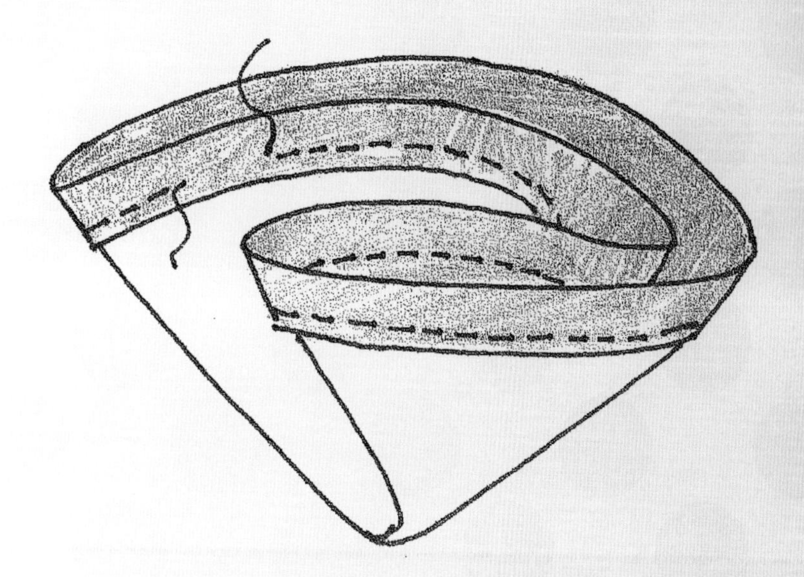

Figure 10

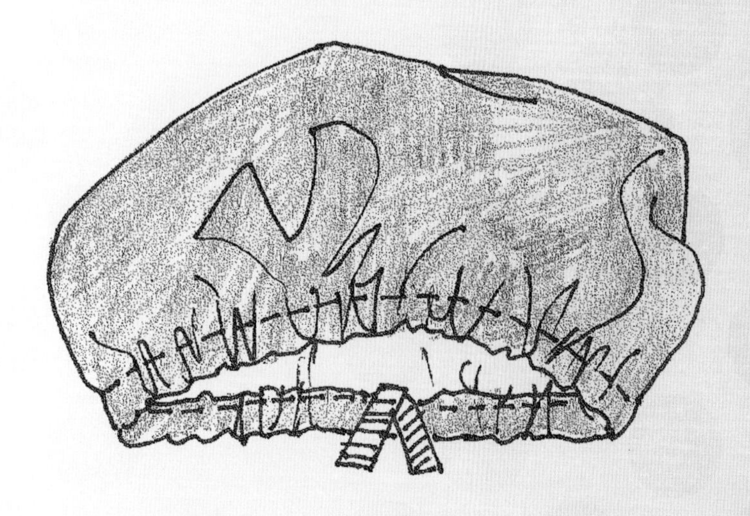

Figure 11

Mask Instructions

1 With right sides together, fold the mask fabric in half widthwise and stitch the short edge. (Figure 12) Turn to the right side and press.

2 Make a pleat in each side of the mask so that the mask now measures 1¾" (4.4cm) wide. Stitch across each side to secure the pleats. (Figure 13)

3 Cut two 30" (76.2cm) pieces of bias tape. Fold each one in half lengthwise and press.

4 Insert the bottom raw edges of the mask into a strip of bias tape and pin, making sure the mask is centered in the tape. Fold the raw ends of the tape ¼" (6mm) to the wrong side and stitch along the whole length of the tape. Repeat with for the other edge of the mask. (Figure 14)

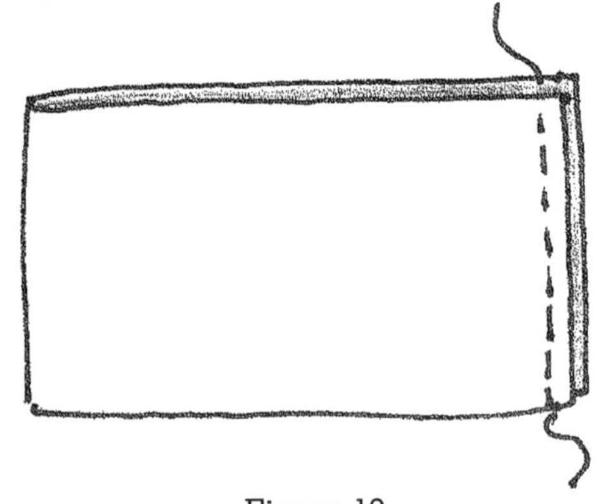

Figure 12

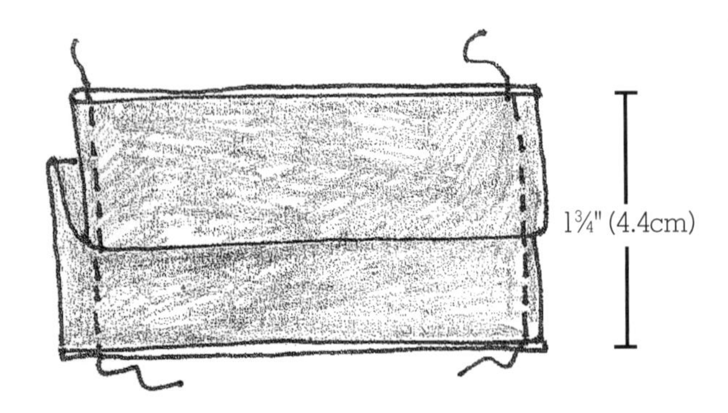

Figure 13

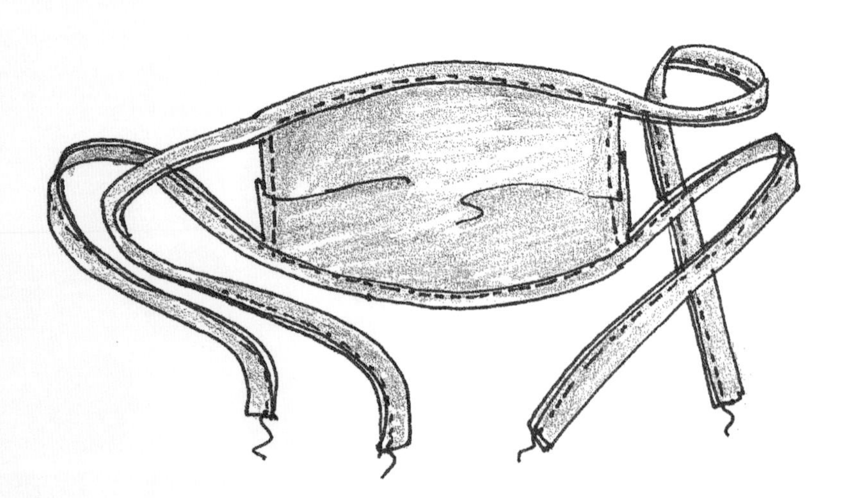

Figure 14

Here's a Hint

This outfit is appropriate for doctors, nurses and other medical personnel. Make this outfit for a child who is sick in the hospital to be a familiar and comforting "caregiver" she can keep at her side at all times. You can choose prints that are similar to the staff in the area where she is being treated, or choose a themed print that features her favorite things such as animals, hearts or princesses. Another idea is to make a lab coat by using the pattern pieces for the Cowgirl Shirt. Extend the length of the front and back pattern pieces, and straighten the hemline. Eliminate the cuffs and extend the sleeves by ¾" (19mm) to achieve the correct look.

Playtime

Gypsy

Blouse, Skirt, Headscarf and Skirt Wrap

Only good fortunes will be told when your doll wears this colorful *Gypsy* costume. The blouse has elastic along the neckline and the sleeves. Bias tape makes the assembly even faster. The tiered skirt is easy to make and is edged with lace. The headscarf and skirt wrap are trimmed with gold coins sold by the yard. The skirt wrap is somewhat bulky, so a snap is used for a closure. If you prefer, tie the ends together. Add lots of shiny jewelry, and your doll will be ready to gaze in a crystal ball.

Blouse Supplies

- *Gypsy* pattern pieces: Blouse Front, Blouse Back, Blouse Sleeve
- ¼ yard (0.2m) solid color fabric
- 1¾ yards (1.6m) pregathered black lace, 1½" (3.8cm) wide
- 16" (40.6cm) bias strip, 1½" (3.8cm) wide or double-fold bias tape
- 18" (45.7cm) elastic, ⅛" (3mm) wide
- 3" (7.6cm) strip of hook and loop tape, cut in half lengthwise

Skirt Supplies

- ⅓ yard (0.3m) print fabric
- 11½" (29.2cm) elastic, ¼" (6mm) wide

Headscarf and Skirt Wrap Supplies

- ¾ yard (0.7m) contrasting fabric
- ¾ yard (0.7m) small coin trim
- 1½ yards (1.4m) large gold coin trim
- 1 large snap
- jewelry finding or button, size 1" (2.5cm)

Blouse Instructions

1 Cut one front, two backs and two sleeves from the solid color fabric following the instructions on the pattern pieces.

2 Press the center back edges ¼" (6mm) to the wrong side. Press another ¼" (6mm) and stitch. With right sides together, sew the sleeves to the front and backs. (Figure 1)

3 Place the wrong side of the black lace to the right side of the blouse along the neckline and baste, turning the ends of the lace ¼" (6mm) to the wrong side. Open out the bias tape and place one long edge of the bias strip along the wrong side of the neckline and stitch. Fold the bias over to the front of the blouse covering the lace heading, tucking in the short ends but not stitching them closed. Stitch along the folded edges to make a casing. Insert a 9½" (24cm) piece of the ⅛" (3mm) elastic through the casing and secure the ends. (Figure 2)

4 Press the lower edges of each sleeve ¼" (6mm) to the wrong side. Press another ¼" (6mm) and stitch close to the edge making a casing. Insert a 4" (10.2cm) piece of the ⅛" (3mm) elastic in each casing and secure the ends. With right sides together, sew the underarm seams. (Figure 3)

5 Press the lower edge of the blouse ¼" (6mm) to the wrong side. Press another ¼" (6mm) and stitch in place.

6 Lapping right over left, sew the hook and loop tape pieces to the back openings.

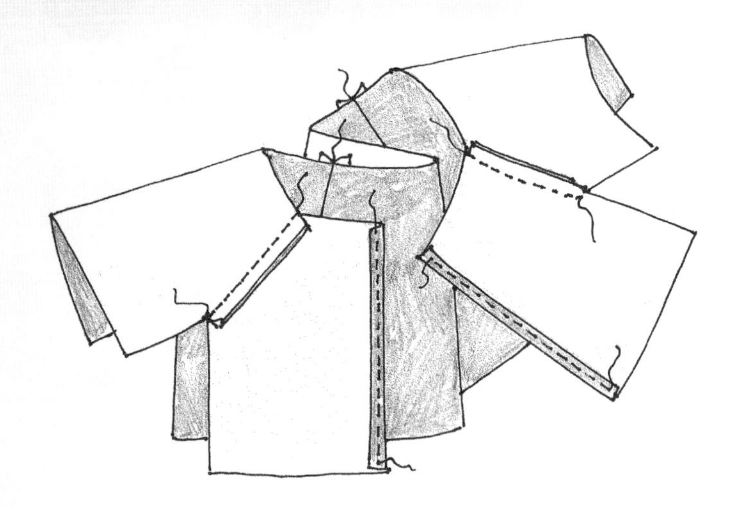

Figure 1

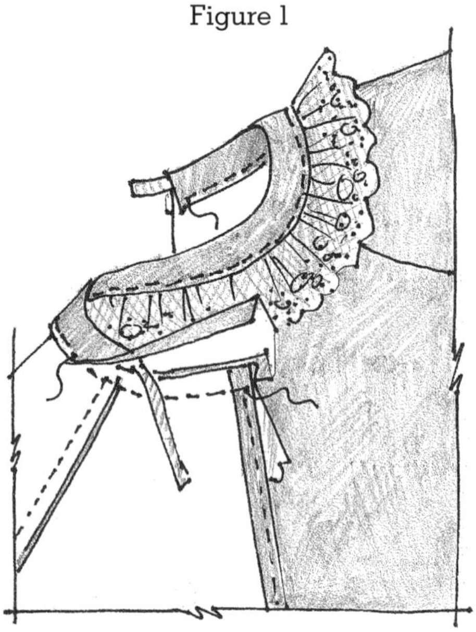

Figure 2

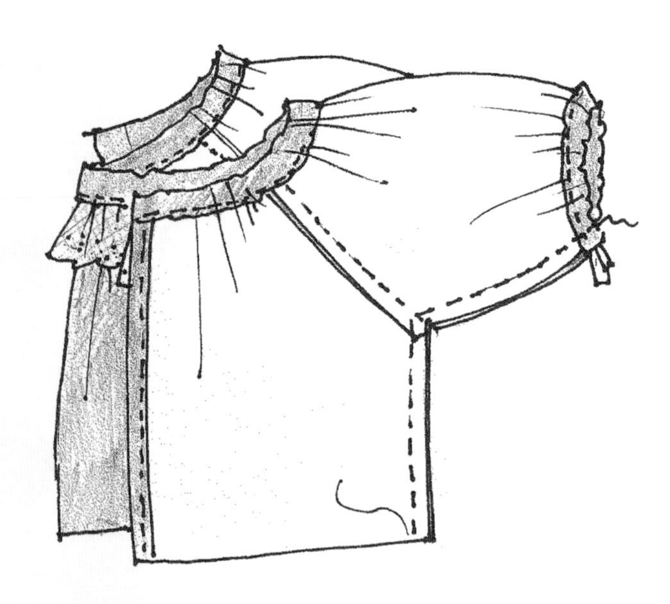

Figure 3

Skirt Instructions

1 Cut three strips of print fabric for the tiers of the skirt. The top tier is 2¾" × 21" (7cm × 53.3cm), the middle tier is 3" × 30" (7.6cm × 76.2cm) and the bottom tier is 3" × 45" (7.6cm × 114.3cm).

2 Press one long edge of the top tier ¼" (6mm) to the wrong side. Press another ½" (13mm) and stitch to make a casing. Set this tier aside.

3 Gather one long edge of the middle tier to measure the same width as the bottom of the top tier. With right sides together, stitch the top and middle tiers together.

4 Press the bottom edge of the bottom tier ¼" (6mm) to the wrong side. Place the remaining black lace underneath the pressed edge and stitch. Gather the other long edge of the bottom tier to measure the same width as the bottom of the middle tier. With right sides together, stitch the bottom and middle tiers together.

5 Insert the ¼" (6mm) elastic in the casing and secure the ends. (Figure 4) With right sides together, sew the center back seam.

Figure 4

Headscarf Instructions

1 Cut a 4" × 27" (10.2cm × 68.6cm) scarf from the contrasting fabric.

2 With right sides together, fold the scarf in half lengthwise. Sew the long edge and one of the short ends. (Figure 5) Turn to the right side and press. Fold the open end ¼" (6mm) to the inside and topstitch.

3 Hand or machine stitch the small gold coins to the stitched long edge of the scarf. (Figure 6)

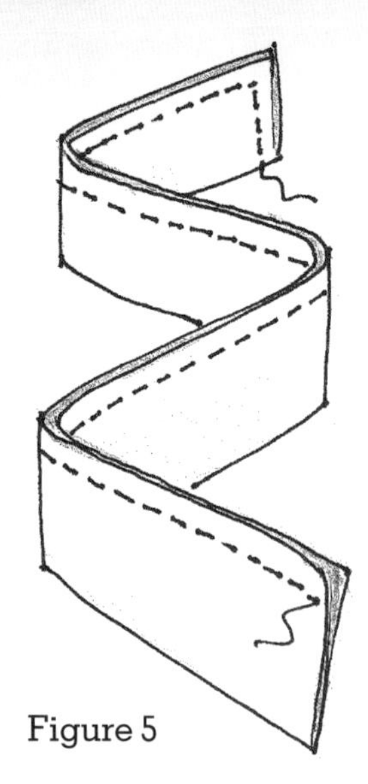

Figure 5

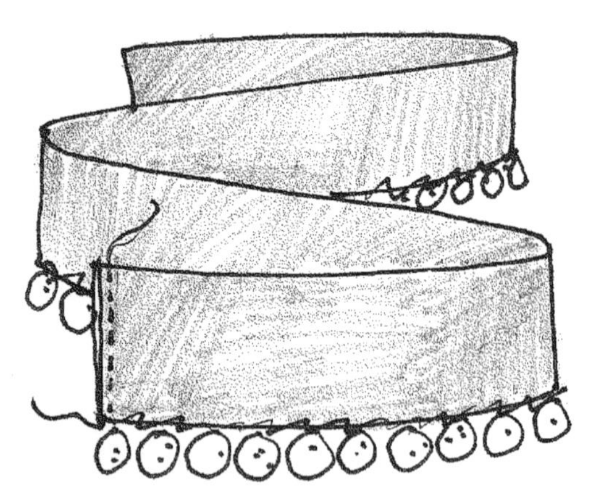

Figure 6

Here's a Hint

This blouse and skirt can be made for your doll's everyday wardrobe. Eliminate the lace on the peasant blouse and pair it with jeans for a very stylish look. The Boho-styled tiered skirt can be made in a variety of current, trendy prints. Just lengthen the lower two tiers to make a fashionable full-length skirt.

Skirt Wrap Instructions

1 Cut a 20" (50.8cm) square of fabric. Press all the edges ¼" (6mm) to the wrong side. Fold the square in half diagonally with wrong sides together.

2 Place the coin trim inside the two pressed edges and stitch in place, pivoting at the corner. (Figure 7)

3 Along the bias edge, measure down 1¾" (4.4cm) and mark a line straight across. Fold the bias edge along this line to the back of the wrap and press. Place the large coin trim under the marked edge and stitch in place. (Figure 8)

4 On the front edge of the wrap, mark another line 1⅝" (4.1cm) down from the bias edge. Fold the edge along the line to the front of the skirt, and topstitch along the upper bias fold to secure in place.

5 Overlap the ends of the wrap and sew the snap 3½" (8.9cm) in from the pointed ends. (Figure 9) Add a button or jewelry finding over the snap.

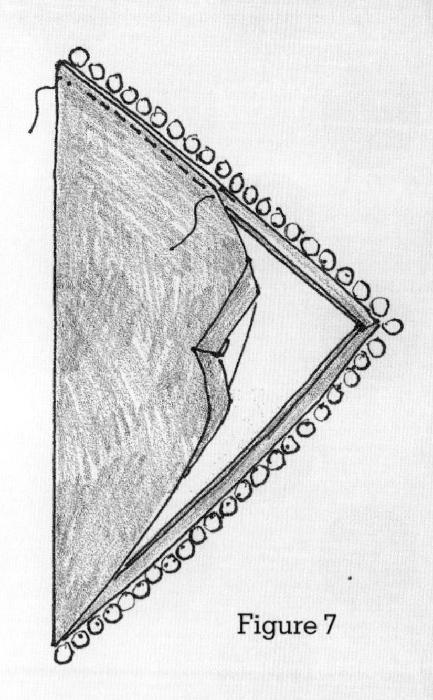

Figure 7

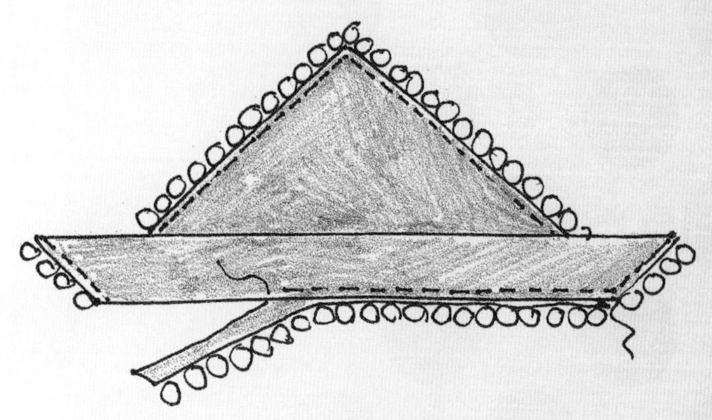

Figure 8

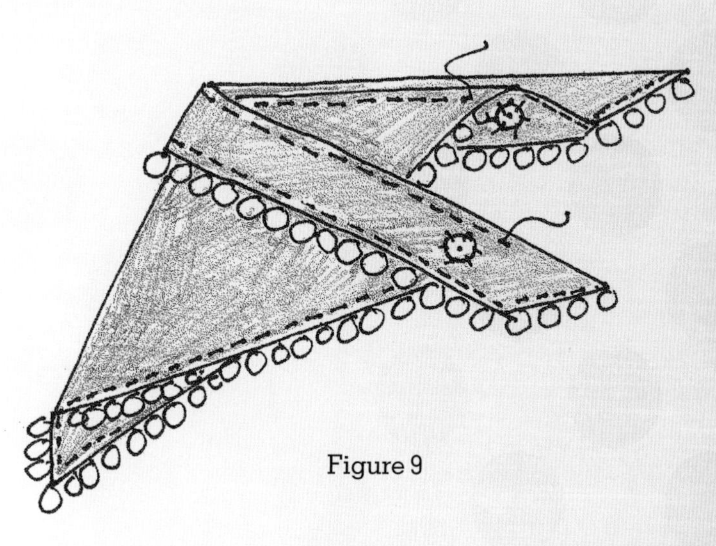

Figure 9

 Published by KP Craft, a division of F+W Media, Inc., 10150 Carver Road, Suite 200, Blue Ash, Ohio 45242. (800) 289-0963. First Edition.

www.fwmedia.com

18 17 16 15 14 5 4 3 2 1

DISTRIBUTED IN CANADA BY FRASER DIRECT
100 Armstrong Avenue
Georgetown, ON, Canada L7G 5S4
Tel: (905) 877-4411

DISTRIBUTED IN THE U.K. AND EUROPE BY F+W MEDIA INTERNATIONAL
Brunel House, Newton Abbot, Devon, TQ12 4PU, England
Tel: (+44) 1626 323200, Fax: (+44) 1626 323319
Email: postmaster@davidandcharles.co.uk

DISTRIBUTED IN AUSTRALIA BY CAPRICORN LINK
P.O. Box 704, S. Windsor NSW, 2756 Australia
Tel: (02) 4577-3555

Edited by Kelly Biscopink
Designed and Photographed by Corrie Schaffeld
Illustrated by Kathy Marsaa
Production coordinated by Greg Nock

ISBN-13: 978-1-4402-3862-8
ISBN-10: 1-4402-3862-6
SRN: U7871

Metric Conversion Chart

to convert	to	multiply by
inches	centimeters	2.54
centimeters	inches	0.4
feet	centimeters	30.5
centimeters	feet	0.03
yards	meters	0.9
meters	yards	1.1

About the Author

As the owner of Fancywork and Fashion, Joan has written sixteen books of doll clothing patterns, as well as two books with machine embroidery and international embellishment ideas. One of her books, *All Dolled Up*, has clothes and accessory patterns for girls and their 18" dolls. Her last book, *Doll Fashion Studio*, has seasonal outfits to make a complete wardrobe for dolls.

In 2011, Joan appeared in a two-part series called "30-Minute Doll Clothes" on *Sewing with Nancy*, featuring doll clothing that can be sewn in 30 minutes or less. She also appeared in a doll clothing series for *Sewing with Nancy* in 2013. Joan enjoys sharing her knowledge of sewing at fabric and quilt shops. Joan and her husband reside in Minnesota and love to travel and experience cultures around the world.

Acknowledgments

I want to sincerely thank the people who helped me bring my vision of this book into print.

First, I want to thank my fabulous illustrator, Kathryn Marsaa, for her talent to draw my instructions with such skill and clarity.

To two creative and talented seamstresses, Amelia Johanson and Sandi Knutie, for their help with garment construction.

To the staff of F&W Media, especially my editor Kelly Biscopink, for their guidance and assistance with this book.

Lastly, to my favorite proofreader, design consultant and traveling companion, my husband Fletcher.

Index